Praise for *Am I Hungry?*

Finally! The truth about losing weight and living a healthy lifestyle. In *Am I Hungry?* Michelle May puts into words what needed to be said for so long: there is no magical quick fix. This is a revolutionary book that offers common-sense solutions for long-term success.
— LEN FROMER, M.D.

Am I Hungry? is a welcome return to sanity in a world gone crazy over diets. This book draws upon what your body already knows to allow you to abandon diets forever and rekindle the normal relationship your body had with food when you were born. I highly recommend this book and the *Am I Hungry?* program to those who have struggled unsuccessfully with diets in the past and want to begin leading a rational life with regard to food and eating.
— MARLO J. ARCHER, PH.D., Licensed Psychologist

In the past my struggle with weight loss has taken so much time and energy. Now *Am I Hungry?* has led me down a completely different path. This approach is so powerful; I know it will change many lives.
— LUPE CAMARGO

Am I Hungry? is the prescription we have all been waiting for—a prescription for healthy living and joy in our own skin!
– EDWARD J. CUMELLA, PH.D., Licensed Psychologist, Director of Research and Education; Remuda Treatment Programs for Anorexia and Bulimia, Inc.

Am I Hungry? is an excellent resource for combining the concept of Intuitive Eating with the principles of good nutrition and healthful living. It drives home the point that dieting and starvation zaps us of our emotional, spiritual, and intellectual energy and causes imbalances. Eating properly, exercising properly, and in general taking care of ourselves, creates a wonderful energy that really balances life and makes it much less difficult and much more fun.
— DEBRA LANDAU-WEST, M.S., R.D.

This book represents a paradigm shift in the way the medical field approaches weight loss. I endorse this method completely and recommend it to all of my patients who are tired of playing the unsuccessful diet game.
— REBECCA MORAN, M.D.

Am I Hungry? is a fresh and intuitive approach for learning how to manage your weight. How wonderful that we already knew everything we need to know but had forgotten because we've been bombarded by fad diets and loads of conflicting information about nutrition—until now! I love that *Am I Hungry?* tosses aside the "good food/bad food" mentality and teaches balance and moderation. We can finally starting living and enjoying food again without the guilt and chains that restrictive diets placed on us.
— DAWN RUTLEDGE, Certified Personal Trainer, Curves Franchisee

The simple lessons of *Am I Hungry?* have changed the way I eat. I have tried many of the popular diets of the past decades but the *Am I Hungry?* principles really make sense and are the keys to making the real changes necessary to reach my health goals.
— RENA HUBER

Am I Hungry? is one of only a handful of books that tell the truth about managing weight. As a childhood obesity and eating disorder specialist, I work with many people who have been given the wrong information, causing them great harm. Turning inside to ask, "Am I hungry?" instead of looking outside to a diet is a much better choice.
— MIA S. ELWOOD, M.S.W., Healthy Futures

I am amazed at what I have learned from *Am I Hungry?* This is truly a life-changing concept—and more importantly, it works!
— FRANCES ACKLEY

As an OB-Gyn that has struggled with my weight for years, I have always known who there was no "quick fix." *Am I Hungry?* has given me hope by transforming the way I look at food—and at life.
— JOEL FALK, M.D.

This team really understands the problems of being overweight and addresses the real reasons people overeat in the first place. *Am I Hungry?* offers strategies and solutions without rules, diets, or gimmicks. It was like reading a good novel. I didn't want to put it down, but I didn't want it to end either. I think many chronic dieters will agree. I can't wait to use it with my clients!
— LINDA STEAKLEY, M.S., R.D., L.D., Author, *FitWeigh* and *Way To Go Kids Nutrition and Fitness Program*

Am I Hungry?

What To Do When Diets Don't Work

Michelle May, M.D.

with
Lisa Galper, Psy.D.
Janet Carr, M.S., R.D.

NOURISH
PUBLISHING

PHOENIX, ARIZONA

www.AmIHungry.com

Am I Hungry? What to Do When Diets Don't Work
Copyright © 2005 by Michelle May, M.D.

Am I Hungry?® is a trademark of Am I Hungry? P.L.L.C.
Please visit our website at www.AmIHungry.com

Book and cover design by Norma Strange, Strange View, Inc.
Fitness illustrations by Bill Riddle, IV

Library of Congress Cataloging-in-Publication Data 2004096088

ISBN 10: 0-9760444-0-4
ISBN 13: 978-0-9760444-0-6

Nourish Publishing
P.O. Box 93686
Phoenix, AZ 85070

IMPORTANT NOTICE: PLEASE READ
In view of the complex, individual nature of health and fitness issues, this book, and the ideas, programs, procedures, and suggestions are not intended to replace the advice of trained medical professionals. All matters regarding one's health require medical supervision.

The authors' roles are strictly educational in the context of the *Am I Hungry?* workshops and materials. They are not providing any medical assessment, individualized therapeutic interventions, or personal medical advice in this context. Seek medical advice from your personal physician regarding your personal risks and benefits insofar as adopting the recommendations of this program.

The authors disclaim any liability arising directly or indirectly from the use of this book or program.

To Owen, Tyler, and Elyse
for showing me in every way that
we are always in this together as a family.

Acknowledgements

From All of Us

We are grateful to so many people for making this book a reality. It is difficult to know where to begin and impossible to know where to end.

We would like to first thank all of our patients and clients for their willingness to trust us with our unconventional approach. We learned as much from them as they learned from us; now their experiences will help transform the lives of others too.

We are indebted to all of those in the non-diet field whose work inspired us to seek a meaningful lifestyle change over ineffective dieting. Their incredible contributions paved the way for this book.

Thank you to Paul St. Onge, M.S. and Loraine Parish, M.S. for their invaluable contributions to the fitness material and extensive literature review, and their heartfelt presence in this book. Our sincere appreciation to Spencer Roberts, M.S, Lettie Lopez, R.D. and many others for their contributions to this program in its infancy. Thank you to our editor Janet Holston, fitness illustrator Bill Riddle IV, and to Norma Strange for sharing our vision and her creative energy in the cover design and interior layout.

Michelle May

I am deeply thankful for my husband Owen and my children Tyler and Elyse for their love, support, and tolerance when this "baby" demanded more than its share of my time and energy. I am also blessed to have four wonderful parents and friends, George and Dixie Shirley and Bill and Janie Riddle. They laid a strong foundation and have continued to lead by love and example.

I thank God for giving me everything and everyone I needed to do this work. Thank you to my many dear friends, colleagues, and other family members who have given so much, whether listening to me speak about it endlessly, reviewing the manuscript, or believing in and encouraging me. And for walking beside me, thank you Marnie Green, Sandi Piedmonte, Dawn Rutledge, Michelle Cunningham and my AAAME classmates and advisors.

Janet Carr

As with many new experiences, being part of writing a book was both exciting and challenging. I could not have made it over the various hurdles without my faithful husband, Doug. Thank you for constantly supporting my efforts, lovingly keeping me on track, and making me laugh when I needed a break.

I'd also like to thank my parents for their belief and support, Linda Steakley for being both mentor and friend, and all of my Remuda Ranch comrades who continue the good fight of spreading a non-diet approach. And mostly, I wish to thank God, for it is by His grace that I am able to accomplish all things.

Lisa Galper

For their incredible mentoring, trust, wisdom, and encouragement, I thank Doris Zachary, Isabel Streisand, Julie Anné, and Patrice Kaiser. To my dear friend Maria Foncellino-Dowling who was the springboard to my career and a steady and loving presence during many difficult times. To Bretta Kennedy and Charee Boulter who have been like sisters to me and have graced my life with so much love and laughter, I am eternally grateful to have you both in my life to inspire me personally and professionally.

I am so thankful for the legacy left to me by my mother, Eileen Galper, whose courage and success has always inspired me. Finally, with deep appreciation of my father Rubin Galper, and my siblings Michele Galper and Steven Galper whose love and support is my anchor.

Table of Contents

Foreword

I have been obese as long as I can remember. I am the son of obese parents and my sister shares this chronic problem. As I look back, I realize that I was not like most of my slim friends: I thought about food all the time. I went to bed each night thinking of what I would eat the next day. Any disappointment, stress, or even success was an excuse to eat more. I had tried many times to lose weight but instead confirmed for myself that diets just weren't the answer. That is why I take the revolutionary yet common sense tenets of *Am I Hungry?* to heart ... and soul.

Like so many physicians, I have cared for countless overweight patients and treated the complications resulting from unhealthy dietary habits and inactive lifestyles. Some of my patients told me openly that they had chosen me as their physician because they felt I couldn't tell them to lose weight since I hadn't been able to do it myself. The issue really hit home when several years ago, after having one kidney removed for renal cell carcinoma, I was diagnosed with high blood pressure and dangerously high cholesterol. I started one, then two, and finally three medications, yet still my blood pressure was out of control. I blamed it on the remaining kidney, but in my heart I knew better. It seemed absurd that after surviving cancer, I hadn't been able to do what was necessary to improve my own health.

A few months before I was to be inaugurated as president of the American Academy of Family Physicians, my wife, Sally, and I were traveling home after visiting our grandchildren. As we talked about my health she asked if I expected to be around to watch our four grandchildren grow up. I thought back to the day in college when I came home to see my grandfather in the hospital after what would be the last of his many heart attacks. I vividly remember his doctor saying, "Mr. Charlie, you have to quit smoking," while crushing out his own cigarette. Had I become that doctor?

When the American Academy of Family Physicians' Commission on Public Health asked if I would be willing to be the "poster boy" for the Academy's AIM (Americans in Motion) fitness initiative, I made the commitment but wondered how I would do what I had never been able to do before. I knew I would have to do it differently this time. This would require a *real* lifestyle change—not just another diet. I had to fundamentally change the way I thought about food, eating, and fitness.

Michelle May, M.D., along with Lisa Galper, Psy.D., and Janet Carr, M.S., R.D. have discovered and written about just such a radical paradigm shift for becoming healthier—*Am I Hungry?* Dr. May's approach is all the more compelling because as a family physician, she has struggled with her weight and has successfully applied this system to her own life. Dr. May's recurring question, *Am I Hungry?* is one of the keys to this rational new approach and represents a significant tool for bringing good health within everyone's reach.

My quest has been successful; so far I have lost over 40 pounds. But more importantly, I have a whole new concept of health and wellness that I can share with my patients. It has become an almost spiritual journey for me, and I have never felt better—or better about *me.* Now, after reading this book, I finally understand what I never could have known all those years ago—that I can take charge of my health and feel happier in the process than I have ever felt before.

I also know that I will, indeed, be there for Thomas, Andrew, Elizabeth, and Patrick; I am confident that Sally and I can enjoy a healthier life because I have learned to ask, *Am I Hungry?*

Michael Fleming, M.D.
Past President, American Academy of Family Physicians

Introduction

Why Should This Time Be Any Different?

You know the feeling. Maybe you have it right now. The one that says, "I can't take it anymore—I just have to lose this weight." Maybe you want to lose a few pounds or maybe you need to lose a lot. Anything may have triggered it: your 20th high school reunion, a Caribbean cruise, feeling winded as you chased your toddler running toward the street. Maybe you have nothing left in your closet that fits, or you felt uncomfortable sitting in a chair with armrests—or you can't even sit in a chair with armrests anymore. Maybe your doctor told you that the reason your knees hurt all the time is that they are carrying a heavier load than they were designed for and your joints are wearing out. Maybe she told you that you have high blood pressure or diabetes, or that you will get one of these conditions if you don't do something about your weight. It could have been any comment or situation, but it became the straw that broke the camel's back.

In a way it is a good feeling. You now have a plan. You feel so determined—this time you will stick to it no matter what. Your friend swears by her method—and she looks great. Or maybe you saw an ad on T.V., read an article in a magazine, or looked in the phone book. The plan seems a little weird or kind of strict but it doesn't matter as long as you can get some of the weight off. You are committed. You have chosen your diet, joined a gym, signed up for a program, or bought the book.

You are finally back in control. You weigh yourself and calculate how long it will take to get to your goal weight. You clean out your refrigerator, your kitchen cabinets, and your desk drawer. You throw away (or finish off) the chips and cookies and start eating celery sticks for snacks. You begin to read labels so you will know what you can eat and what you shouldn't. You take your lunch to work every day and try new healthy recipes on your family. ("Oh no, Mom's on a diet again!") You drink your eight glasses of water every day. You buy new walking shoes and get up early almost every morning. You feel great!

The weight starts to come off. Maybe that first week you lose three or four pounds. Never mind that part of it was water or even muscle. You already feel thinner—and a little smug. As you watch the others in the break room scarfing down donuts you think, "If they had self-control and willpower like me, they would know how bad those things are for them and they could resist them too." Eventually someone notices you are losing weight so you tell them about your new diet. They tell you about the one that worked for them and everyone within earshot chimes in with a favorite diet story or two. Eventually the conversation shifts to food and recipes and eating—a favorite theme in any gathering.

But one day you weigh in again and you haven't lost as much as you think you should. You vow to try harder, and you do. In the back of your mind a little voice says, "This isn't worth it." At first you remind yourself about all of the reasons you need to lose weight so you ignore the voice and keep going— maybe for another day, maybe for another year. But that little voice gets louder. You see someone eating ice cream and the voice says, "It's not fair." One morning you wake up early for your walk, but you feel too tired and the voice says, "This is too hard."

You buy a bag of candy at the store and the voice says, "It's for the kids." You put it away in the cabinet but the little voice says, "You have been so good, you can have one piece." You eat one piece and you can't believe how wonderful it tastes and the voice says, "You can walk a little extra tomorrow, have another one." You eat one more, then another, and before you know it, half the bag is gone. Maybe it was a little bag or maybe it was a large bag; the point is you weren't supposed to eat it. So the voice says, "You already blew it. You might as well eat the rest so you won't be tempted when you go back on your diet tomorrow. Besides, how are you going to explain half a bag of candy?" So you finish the bag.

Then the voice changes. It is not a little voice anymore; it has become loud and cruel. The voice says, "I can't believe you did that after how hard you have worked! You couldn't stick to it, just like all the other times." So you vow to be good tomorrow. And you are, at first. But something has changed. You don't feel like you are in control anymore. You now know that you are just one piece of candy away from going right back to where you started. And the voice screams, "You are a loser!"

Before long, whatever motivated you in the first place doesn't seem that important anymore. Your willpower fades and the voice whispers, "Maybe next time it will be different." So you go back to eating like you did before. It's over, for now anyway. Because eventually, something will happen to give you that feeling again, the one that says, "I can do it this time." The roller coaster starts up the hill for another ride.

But this time, you are holding *this* book. *Am I Hungry?* Maybe your doctor told you about it, or you heard about it on a talk show, or your friend claims it changed her life. That sounds good. *Too* good. The little voice says, "You have been on this ride before. Why should this one be any different? You know you won't be able to do it."

You *can* do it, because this book is different. In fact, it may even seem a bit *too* different. Your little voice says, "No dieting? How is that going to help? You are already out of control. What you really need is willpower and some strict guidelines to whip you back into shape."

Yet that hasn't worked for you—or most people—in the past, so why do you keep going back to the same old thing camouflaged by a different name and a different set of rules? Deep down inside, don't you believe there has to be another way?

There is. In fact, you may be surprised to learn that the answers have been within your reach the whole time. The problem is that you have been reaching *out* instead of reaching in.

To be clear, this book is not going to give you a whole new set of rules to follow. In fact, we recommend only one "rule": Whenever you have an urge to eat, ask yourself, "Am I hungry?" Sounds simple? It is. But it is not always easy. In a way, it would be easier to just do what someone else tells you, than to really dig down inside and find the answers for yourself. But we believe that this is the only way.

To answer the simple question, "Am I hungry?" you will need to become aware, not only of your physical state, but aware of your thoughts and feelings too. You will need to restore the skills you were born with and develop new tools necessary for lifelong weight management and health. That is why you are holding *this* book *this* time.

Am I Hungry? is not just a book. It is a *multidimensional system*, a series of integrated processes, because the solution to managing your weight is more complex than simply knowing what to eat and how much to exercise. This multidimensional system combines expertise in the medical, nutritional, and behavioral aspects of weight management. An otherwise complicated process has been broken into a series of simple steps that can be mastered one manageable piece at a time.

Let us emphasize that this will be a *process*, a new learning process, so don't let that little voice tell you that you have to do this perfectly or not at all. You do not need to do it perfectly for it to be effective. In fact, you will make many mistakes along the way—we still do. This will also be a very personal process. Every choice you make is a learning opportunity, a chance to better understand why you do the things you do and how to do them differently next time. Be kind and patient with yourself; the rewards are well worth it.

The first section of each chapter, Decision Points, will guide you through the Am I Hungry? system by asking simple questions to increase your awareness of what you are thinking, feeling, and doing. You will build layers of important weight management skills and healthier ways of nourishing your body, your mind, and your soul—without dieting.

As you let go of restrictive and complicated diet rules, you will need a solid foundation of nutrition and fitness information to help you make the best possible choices for your health. The Fitness and Nutrition sections of each chapter will teach you the essentials of these topics and provide you with the motivation you need to create your own personalized plan for building optimal health.

You may be tempted to skip over the fitness and nutrition sections, believing that you have heard it all before. However, the information that you have been given in the past may have been inaccurate, confusing, or tainted with diet messages like "eating fat is bad" or "exercise helps burn off calories when you cheat." You may also be afraid that this is where we will slip in rules for you to follow. We won't. These sections will help you focus on one aspect of fitness and nutrition at a time to help you make important step-by-step adjustments to your personal plan. These small, focused changes are probably very different from the "all or nothing" approach you may have taken in the past, but as one of our participants said, "I have learned so much about taking good care of myself. It happened so gradually, that it didn't hurt a bit. In fact, it changed my life!"

We have walked this journey with thousands of people. Throughout this book, you will hear some of their stories. Some are almost word for word, while others are composites of several people with similar experiences. They will help us illustrate important points. But most of all, we hope they will help you see that you are not alone. This is Michelle May's story:

> Michelle was chubby from an early age. Picture red hair, lots of freckles—and chubby. She was told that there were starving children in Africa, so her plate had to be cleaned. She had an athletic, skinny younger brother who could, and would, eat anything not nailed down—so she also had to make sure to get her share first. Soon after her

parents divorced, a girl at her new dance school teased her about being fat, so she quit taking lessons.

Since she was the smart one, not the athletic one—she spent most of her free time just hanging around with her friends. They snacked to chase away boredom and she gained more weight. She also discovered that food was great for relieving stress, at least for a little while. In the long run though, it became a major source of stress for her. Subtle and not-so-subtle comments and embarrassing shopping trips to find clothes made it clear that she had to do something. The stage was set.

For the next twenty-five years, Michelle was on one diet after another. She had her favorite—the one that worked for her as long as she stuck to it. She also discovered that exercise helped too—as long as she stuck to it. But it was hard to stick to any of them for very long. She developed features of an eating disorder that helped her cope with her painful relationship with food.

Ironically, despite the fact that she couldn't stick to a diet forever, she had little trouble getting through college, medical school, and residency, and eventually found herself in the position of advising her patients to lose weight. Most of them didn't seem to fare any better than she had. That was little consolation.

She felt discouraged and ashamed. How do you help someone do something you haven't been able to do yourself? She knew it was time to try again but it didn't seem fair— her husband and children never dieted and they never struggled with their weight. In fact, they ate whatever they wanted, but they rarely ate more than they needed.

Did they just have a better metabolism? That was probably part of it. She knew hers was a mess after years of overeating and dieting. Did they have more willpower? No. It seemed unlikely that they would have been able to follow a diet for very long either. But there was something else, something fundamentally different about the way they *thought about food. In fact, they didn't really think about food at all—unless they were hungry.*

Could the answer really be that obvious? Could she learn to listen to hunger again to guide her eating? Her little voice said, "I really don't want to go on another diet. Let's try it their way this time."

It was surprisingly simple, but it was not always easy. After years of trying to follow other people's rules about food, ignoring hunger, and eating for all sorts of other reasons, it was difficult to trust her body and her instincts. But she created a new path for herself and developed a system to manage her weight that really worked.

And something else completely unexpected happened along the way. She discovered parts of herself she had lost, or did not even know existed. She found health, happiness, and wholeness. She also discovered a purpose for her life and a passion for helping others find their paths to wholeness too.

Enjoy *your* journey!

Michelle May, M.D.
Lisa Galper, Psy.D.
Janet Carr, M.S., R.D.

A Note to our Colleagues in the Medical and Health Professions

If you have ever felt frustrated when trying to help your patients and clients manage their weight and motivate them to live a healthier lifestyle, this book is for you. The truth is, if diets were effective for long-term weight management, their problem would have been solved with their first one. An important first step toward really making a difference is understanding why diets haven't worked for most of them in the first place.

With diets, the latest diet "expert" defines which foods are "bad" and therefore which foods must be avoided, limited, or counted. To comply, dieters must maintain their willpower indefinitely. Not surprisingly, dieters often exhibit an increased preoccupation with food and feelings of deprivation, leading to a love-hate relationship with food.

The expert also determines when, what, and how much dieters should eat, regardless of their intrinsic hunger and fullness cues. This doesn't allow them to learn to use their innate ability to manage their weight. Dieting may backfire, leading to a decrease in a dieter's metabolism. In the end, most people regain their lost weight—and sometimes more.

Furthermore, the expert often prescribes exercise to burn off fat or earn the right to eat. In essence, exercise becomes a punishment for eating. A common result of this negative association is that when the diet is over, the exercise program is usually over too.

Most importantly, diets focus on *what* people should eat without addressing why they are eating in the first place. Dieters often don't learn to recognize and effectively cope with their eating triggers and meet their true bio-psycho-social needs.

In short, dieting is negative, disempowering, and unsustainable. In its wake, the dieter is often left with feelings of guilt, disappointment, lowered self-esteem, and diminished self-efficacy. This becomes a downward cycle from which they may never physically or emotionally recover.

Yet many in the health and fitness arena continue to advocate dieting despite a failure rate that would be considered unacceptable for most other therapeutic interventions. At what point will society begin to doubt the wisdom of the diets rather than the fortitude of the dieters?

Granted, this requires a paradigm shift. Dieting is so pervasive in society today that it is difficult to imagine it any other way. But there is a growing non-diet movement that has been largely unheard, misunderstood, or dismissed by the medical community. Faced with a burgeoning epidemic of overweight and obesity, can we afford to ignore it any longer?

It is time to move away from promoting ineffective dieting and instead guide people to relearn their instinctive ability to feed themselves an appropriate amount of food. We need to help them recognize and find ways to meet their other needs in other ways. Further, they deserve a solid foundation of legitimate, reliable nutrition information and freedom from the harsh, arbitrary limits of restrictive dieting. Just as important, they need a positive, sustainable approach to fitness in order to build an enjoyable, healthy, active lifestyle.

Am I Hungry? addresses all of these issues in an innovative, integrated, multidimensional, and personalized approach simply not found among the quick-fix diets predominant today.

You have our pledge that in these pages, you will find common sense instead of gimmicks, a positive approach to eating and activity, and lifelong skills in lieu of quick fix schemes. *Am I Hungry?* can transform a person who struggles with weight and eating issues into a person with healthy attitudes and behaviors. You and those you care for will gain a whole new approach to weight—and life—management.

Wishing you wisdom, joy, and optimal health,

Michelle May, M.D.
Lisa Galper, Psy.D.
Janet Carr, R.D., M.S.

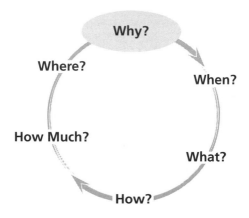

CHAPTER 1

Decision Point: Why Do I Eat?

Am I hungry? This deceptively simple question can be the key to ending your struggle with weight and food—*without* dieting. Essential to survival, hunger is your cue to take care of your body's natural and fundamental need for energy and nutrients. If you are frustrated with your weight or struggle with making food choices, you may not be using this basic skill to determine when, what, and how much to eat.

Here are comments from people who came to us for help with their weight and food issues. Do any of these statements sound familiar?

- I am hungry all the time.
- I am never hungry.
- I can't tell when I am hungry.
- I know I am not hungry but I eat anyway.
- I am starving by the time I eat, so I'll eat anything I can get my hands on.
- I eat by the clock.

- I think about food all of the time.
- I have trouble stopping myself when I eat "bad" foods.
- I often eat until I am uncomfortable.
- I have tried a lot of diets.
- I don't have enough willpower to stick to a diet.
- I love food and eating too much to reach a healthy weight.
- I sometimes ignore hunger in order to control my weight.
- I feel guilty about eating certain foods.
- I am confused about what I should be eating.
- I am either dieting or eating too much.
- I am an emotional eater.
- I use food to cope with stress and other feelings.
- I have a love-hate relationship with food.
- I dread the thought of dieting but I don't know what else to do.

If you struggle with your weight or your eating habits, you may be having difficulty listening to your own internal signals of hunger and satiety. *Hunger* is your body's signal that it needs nourishment, while *satiety* is your body's signal that it does not need food. How a person responds to these signals often separates those who have difficulty with their weight from those who seem to eat whatever they want and maintain a healthy weight.

Your Eating Cycle

To understand why hunger and satiety are so important, consider the differences between people who don't struggle with their weight, people who are overweight, and people who are always on a diet. What characteristics and traits do these different groups of people have? Why do they eat? What role does food serve in their lives? Think of their eating patterns— what, how often, and how much do they eat? How physically active are they?

Certainly, people are various sizes and shapes, have genetically different metabolisms, and have different levels of activity. But many of the people in these groups share common characteristics. We refer to these different eating styles as Instinctive Eating, Over Eating, and Restrictive Eating.

Instinctive Eating: First, think of people who stay within their healthy weight range naturally. Try to picture people who seem to do this effortlessly, rather than people who appear to exert incredible willpower and self-control. Perhaps you are thinking of your spouse, a friend, a child, or even yourself—before you began gaining weight or struggling with food. These are people who stay slim without a great deal of effort.

Angie and Tom eat when they are hungry and stop eating when they are satisfied. They don't think or talk about food all of the time. They take gourmet-cooking classes together and really enjoy eating just about whatever they want. However, they don't have any trouble turning down even delicious food when they aren't hungry. They seem to have a lot of energy; they play in a softball league and love hiking on the weekends. Their weights remain stable, going up and down in a narrow range. They never diet but are willing to make changes in the way they eat if they learn new information that will improve their health. Angie and Tom don't really know what they do to stay slim. They have difficulty understanding why overweight people can't just stop overeating.

Over Eating: Now think about people who are overweight—maybe you or someone you know well. Two people we worked with are typical of many others with weight struggles.

Alicia and Paul are both overweight and are starting to worry about their health. Their doctor told them that Alicia's blood sugar was too high and that Paul had developed high blood pressure. Alicia and Paul think and talk about food, eating, and dieting all the time. Alicia and Paul admit that they are not really aware of their hunger.

Alicia says she can't tell when she's hungry but Paul says he's always hungry. They eat because it is mealtime or because something looks good—whether they are hungry or not. They joke that they are star members of the clean plate club and that the all-you-can-eat buffet loses money on them. They often feel stuffed after a meal—yet they still manage to eat dessert. They reward, comfort, and entertain themselves by eating. Alicia and Paul both say they feel guilty and out of control around food. They experiment with the latest fad diets, but they always end up cheating and giving up. Of course, that makes them feel bad, especially since they usually end up gaining even more weight than they lost. They don't feel very healthy and complain of feeling tired all the time. Exercise is hard for them and they tend to think of it as a punishment for their overeating. They think slim people have more willpower and better metabolisms than they do.

Restrictive Eating: Now think of people who always seem to be on a diet. You may know a lot of people like this—people who manage to keep their weight down by chronically restricting their eating and exercising compulsively.

Karen drives her husband Mark crazy because she is always struggling to lose those last ten pounds. She weighs herself daily, sometimes more than once a day. Most of the time, she thinks she is too fat no matter how much she weighs. The numbers on the scale often determine how her day goes. Since she is always trying to lose weight, she often won't allow herself to eat—even when she is hungry. She disconnects from her hunger by eating only predetermined amounts and types of food at specific times, depending on the rules of the diet she is following. Karen seems preoccupied with thoughts of food; in fact, she thinks about it all the time. She worries a lot about what she should or shouldn't be eating. Mark teases her that she doesn't eat real food—just their chemically altered diet-friendly versions. Secretly, she sometimes eats a "bad" food and ends up overeating or bingeing on it. This reinforces in her mind that dieting is the only way to maintain control over her urges to eat those "forbidden" foods. She punishes herself for cheating by starving herself later or forcing herself to exercise more. She rarely misses her daily exercise regimen because she worries that she will gain weight. Karen thinks Mark should have as much self-control and willpower as she does.

Do you recognize your eating style in one or more of these descriptions? Let's take a closer look at each one using The Eating Cycle. The Eating Cycle is a way of understanding how you make conscious or subconscious decisions about eating, and how each decision affects the other decisions you make. Each Decision Point in the cycle represents a choice that you as an eater make about consuming food and burning it as fuel.

The Eating Cycle

Why? Why do I eat? In other words, what drives my Eating Cycle?

Why?
Why do I eat?

Where?
Where does my energy go?

When?
When do I want to eat?

Eating Cycle

How Much?
How much do I eat?

What?
What will I eat?

How?
How do I eat?

When? When do I want to eat? When do I think about eating and when do I decide to eat?

What? What will I eat? What food do I choose from all of the available options? What do I decide to fuel my body with?

How? How do I eat? How, specifically, do I eat the food that I have chosen?

How Much? How much do I eat? How much fuel do I give my body when I eat?

Where? Where does my energy go? Once I have chosen and eaten the food to fuel my body with, where do I spend that energy?

The Instinctive Eating Cycle

Why? The Cycle Driver is hunger. When you are in an Instinctive Eating Cycle, hunger is your primary cue for eating. When your body needs food, it triggers the sensation of hunger. Hunger guides you to decide when and how much to eat.

When? When you are hungry. Your body lets you know it needs fuel by sending you hunger signals. Once you recognize

the need for fuel, you must decide whether to eat depending on the circumstances, your preferences, the availability of food, convenience, and other factors.

What? Whatever you choose. You are able to select food from all of the available options to fuel your body. Your food choices are affected by your preferences, your awareness of nutrition information, and what foods are available. In the Instinctive Eating Cycle, strict diets aren't used to decide what to eat and food does not hold any particular power over you.

How? You eat intentionally. When you are in an Instinctive Eating Cycle, you eat with purpose. Usually that purpose is to satisfy hunger but even when the purpose is enjoyment, eating holds your attention so you are able to experience the maximal pleasure.

How Much? You eat enough to satisfy hunger. You decide how much food to eat by how hungry you are, how filling the food is, how soon you will be eating again, and other factors. When your hunger is satisfied you stop eating—even if there is food left. You recognize that being too full is uncomfortable and unnecessary.

Where? Your energy goes toward living your life. As you go about your day, your body freely uses the food you ate for the fuel it needs during work, play, exercise, and even rest. Any leftover fuel is stored until it is needed. Once your readily available fuel is depleted or stored, the symptoms of hunger develop, triggering a desire to eat, and the cycle repeats itself.

The Over Eating Cycle

Why? The Over Eating Cycle is driven by triggers. Eating in response to these triggers may give you temporary pleasure or distraction. For example, if the trigger was sadness, food may be temporarily soothing and distracting from the source of sadness. Likewise, if the trigger was a big tray of brownies, eating several of them would be pleasurable. The distraction or pleasure is initially satisfying and therefore drives the Over Eating Cycle.

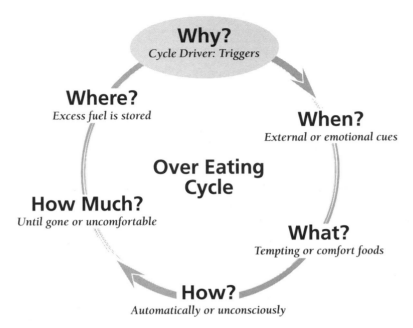

When? The desire to eat is often triggered by various environmental and emotional triggers. External cues, such as the time of day, appetizing food, or certain activities associated with food may trigger your urges to eat. The trigger may also be emotions such as loneliness, boredom, anger, or stress. Sometimes hunger triggers the initial urge to eat, but then environmental and emotional cues trigger overeating.

What? The types of food you choose to eat in response to triggers other than hunger are more likely to be tempting foods or comfort foods. For example if the trigger was a ballgame, the choice may be a hot dog and chips; if the trigger was stress, the choice might be chocolate or cookies. It is less likely that you will choose nutritious foods in the Over Eating Cycle since you are not eating in response to your body's physical needs.

How? In the Over Eating Cycle, you are more likely to eat automatically and/or unconsciously. You may eat, or continue to eat, whether you are hungry or not. For example, you may grab a handful of candy or nuts from a bowl as you pass by. You may eat while you are distracted watching T.V., driving, or talking on the phone. You may eat secretly or quickly to finish before

someone catches you. Additionally, if you feel guilty about
eating, you can't fully enjoy the food you choose. Eating in this
way cannot be physically or emotionally satisfying.

How Much? You might eat until the food is gone or you feel
uncomfortable. When you are in an Over Eating Cycle, the
amount of food you eat is often determined by external factors
like how much food is served or how much is in the package. If
your body didn't give you the start-eating signal (hunger), the
only stop-eating signal is discomfort, running out of food, or
being interrupted. All too often, you will feel full,
uncomfortable, or even numb after eating, instead of feeling
content and satisfied.

Where? Any excess fuel is stored. The fuel you consumed
goes toward living your life; however, if you eat when your body
didn't signal its need for fuel with hunger, your body has no
choice but to store the extra fuel for later in the form of body
fat. When you eat in response to external and emotional triggers
the distraction is temporary and the pleasure is soon replaced by
discomfort since you didn't really need the food in the first
place. Eating this way and therefore carrying extra body fat can
trigger negative emotions that may lead to more overeating.
When your true needs have not been met, the Over Eating Cycle
will continue.

The Restrictive Eating Cycle

Why? In Restrictive Eating, the cycle is driven by rules that
determine when, what, and how much to eat. The rules may
come from an "expert" or may be self-imposed by the dieter.
When you are in a Restrictive Eating Cycle, the number on the
scale or how well you have been following the rules may
determine how you feel about yourself on a particular day.

When? The rules determine whether or not you are allowed
to eat, for example, "Eat six small meals a day" or "Don't eat after
6 p.m." Often the rules were created for a reasonable purpose. In
the examples above, eating frequent meals may prevent you from
getting hungry, so theoretically, your eating will be easier to
control. Prohibiting eating in the evening prevents eating due to

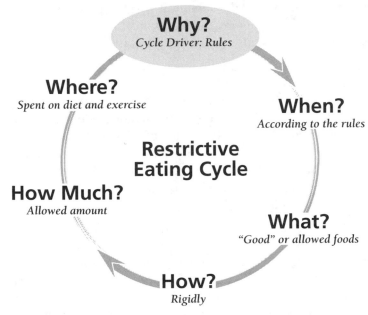

environmental triggers like watching television. However, these rules place artificial constraints on your eating that don't necessarily honor your body's natural hunger rhythms—and of course they don't address the reasons you want to eat in the first place.

What? You must eat "good" foods that are allowed on the diet. You may need to resist your favorite foods or even avoid certain situations if there are too many forbidden foods that you would be tempted to eat. In the Restrictive Eating Cycle, choosing the right food is very important because when the choice is good, you are good. But when the choice is bad, you are bad.

How? Following the rules may require you to be very structured or even rigid in your eating. However, always having to choose good foods may cause you to feel deprived, while choosing bad foods may cause you to feel guilty.

How Much? You eat the allowed amount since the quantity of food is predetermined by the rules. This may require weighing, measuring, counting, or in some way using an external means to determine how much food you can have or how much food must be eaten. The purpose of these rules is to prevent you from choosing too much food, or perhaps not eating enough, on the assumption that you do not have the ability to consume an appropriate amount of food without following a set of rules.

Where? The Restrictive Eating Cycle usually requires a great deal of mental and emotional energy. Just as in the Instinctive Eating Cycle, your body will use whatever fuel it needs for work, play, exercise, and rest. However, if you are significantly under-eating, your body may attempt to conserve as much fuel as possible by decreasing your metabolism. Furthermore, while exercise is very important for overall health and fitness, in Restrictive Eating, exercise is sometimes used to earn the "right" to eat or to punish yourself for overeating or for eating a "bad" food. While it may appear to others that you are just trying to be healthier, many of your thoughts and behaviors may revolve around food and exercise.

Hunger is Your Primitive Instinct

The key distinction between these three eating styles is that in Over Eating, you are "out of control"; in Restrictive Eating, you are "in control"; but in Instinctive Eating, you are "in charge." Since hunger and your need for fuel drives the Instinctive Eating Cycle, you are in charge of how you will best nourish your body and soul. To understand why this is so important, let's take a closer look at hunger.

Hunger and the instinctual drive to satisfy hunger are essential for survival. Hunger is a primitive yet reliable way of signaling your body's need for food, and therefore, regulating your nutritional intake. The sensations of hunger and satiety are the simplest, yet most powerful tools available to you for reconnecting with your instinctive ability to know what your body needs.

You were born with the ability to know the answer without even asking the question, "Am I hungry?" If you have cared for or observed infants and young children, you know that it is difficult to make them eat when they are not hungry—and it is almost impossible to deal with them when they need to eat. Instinctively, babies cry to let their caregivers know when they are hungry. Toddlers in perpetual motion manage to eat only small amounts of food but eat frequently enough to meet their needs. Young children have the innate ability to regulate their eating according to what their bodies require. During periods of rapid growth or activity, children may be hungry all the time; when their calorie requirements decrease, they lose interest in food.

How You Learned to Ignore Hunger

Unfortunately, internal and external influences may cause this natural system of regulating food intake to go awry. For example, if a caregiver feeds a baby to calm every cry, the baby will learn that eating can soothe any discomfort. Once a child is old enough to sit at the table, a well-intentioned parent, wanting the child to eat a well-balanced diet, will serve the amount of food he or she thinks the child needs. The parent will then try to force the child to eat everything that has been served by saying, "clean your plate." This teaches the child to ignore the physical discomfort of being too full in order to comply with the parent's expectations and win parental approval. Sometimes the parent's pressure to eat certain types and amounts of food backfires and the dinner table can become a battleground of intense power struggles.

The child that doesn't get dessert unless he or she finishes all their dinner learns that sweets are an incentive to eat more than their body was hungry for. "Eat all of your dinner if you want dessert" translates to "You must overeat so I will reward you by letting you overeat some more." Children have a natural desire for sweet and higher fat foods but using sweets to reward good behavior or bribe them into finishing their whole meal can cause children to believe that these foods are special and make them want to eat them even more.

Although meeting the basic nutritional needs of children is critical, it is important to provide meals and snacks in a way that respects the child's hunger and fullness cues. If not, the stage is set for food and weight problems in the future.

Children and adults may also learn to eat in response to environmental and emotional triggers. If you are eating when you are not hungry, you must be eating for other reasons. The triggers are different for each person and at various times, but if you struggle with your weight, it is likely that you are sometimes eating food for reasons other than satisfying hunger.

For example, have you ever suddenly become hungry when you walked by the doughnuts in the break room at work? It is common for people to confuse this sudden urge to eat with true hunger, but environmental situations like this often trigger this reaction whether your body needs food or not. Other environmental triggers include mealtimes, holidays, advertisements, entertainment activities, social situations, people, places, and even just stepping on a scale or thinking about starting another diet. There are hundreds of specific examples, but the availability of calorically dense, appealing foods in increasingly larger portions is a problem for individuals and society.

Further, many people learn to use food to cope with emotions. For example, if you have had a stressful day, you may comfort or reward yourself by eating a large bowl of ice cream. All people have emotional connections with food, including celebrating special events, expressing love, or finding comfort in Grandma's apple pie. However, emotional eating becomes destructive when it is the primary way that a person copes with feelings such as loneliness, boredom, anger, stress, or depression. To be clear, this does not imply that you are psychologically disturbed if you have food or weight struggles. It simply means you may have learned to cope with certain emotions by eating and therefore, at times you use food for purposes other than energy and nourishment.

When people become frustrated with their weight, they often turn to diets to solve their problems. Most diets have very specific rules about food choices and exercise but ironically, you may have to ignore hunger cues in order to follow the rules. As a result, dieting moves you even further from your ability to know what your body really needs.

Most diets focus on what people should or should not be eating and overlook the fact that many people eat in response to triggers other than hunger. Since food is often not being consumed to satisfy the need for fuel, focusing on the form of the fuel is not very effective in the long run—but that is what most diets do.

Can people who are out of touch with their hunger signals begin to recognize and use hunger again to learn to eat instinctively? Definitely! Hunger is a natural, innate tool. The skills for using that tool effectively can be relearned in order to reach and maintain a healthier weight without dieting. Instead of following strict rules created by "experts," you can become the expert on meeting your needs. This book will teach you how to use the fundamental information delivered by your hunger cues to determine when, what, and how much you need to eat.

Which Cycle Are You In?

As you read this, you probably recognized that you follow different eating cycles at different times. Even people who usually eat instinctively may eat in response to environmental triggers like a birthday party or an emotional trigger like stress. People who predominately overeat or eat restrictively also eat to satisfy hunger at times. However, though they may eat instinctively at times, if they predominantly eat in response to triggers or often restrict their eating, they may find it difficult to reach and maintain their natural weight.

People who struggle with food and their weight are usually not aware that they are caught in an Over Eating or Restrictive Eating Cycle. They often feel stuck and powerless to change—without understanding why.

When you have been eating too much you may not recognize that you are caught in a vicious Over Eating Cycle that literally feeds on itself. As you eat in response to your triggers, the temporary distraction or pleasure you get can act like an engine that drives the cycle. You may decide that dieting is the only way to stop overeating and gain control over your eating habits and your weight. However, dieting simply switches you into a Restrictive Eating Cycle.

While in a Restrictive Eating Cycle, you may continue to eat in response to your triggers, but now you choose foods that are allowed on the diet. For example, you may eat to decrease stress but choose veggies to munch on instead of chips. As a result, your trigger hasn't changed and you still aren't effectively coping with the stress. Additionally, you may continue to overeat the allowed foods, expending a great deal of energy figuring out how to get the most food while staying within the confines of the diet.

Over time, you may begin to feel deprived or worn out by all of the time and energy it takes to follow the rules in a Restrictive Eating Cycle. So you cheat, feel guilty, and give up, shifting back into an Over Eating Cycle, once again consuming your favorite foods in response to the triggers that were never effectively dealt with. It is common for people to shift repeatedly from one cycle to the other. This cycle switching is also known as yo-yo dieting.

On the other hand, the Instinctive Eating Cycle is a more natural pattern of eating that meets your natural need for energy and nutrients. When you are in an Instinctive Eating Cycle you simply don't think about food or eating very much unless you are hungry. You don't obsess over food because you don't need to. Instead, you trust your body to let you know if and when you need food, and how much you should eat. If you are exposed to food when you are not hungry you may take a passing interest in it but you won't choose to eat a significant amount of it because you know you would feel uncomfortable afterward. You can eat anything you want when you are hungry, so you don't have to spend a lot of time deciding in advance what you are going to eat. You can truly enjoy food and eating because you won't feel physically or emotionally uncomfortable after you eat. You can consciously choose to follow a healthier diet, but you don't expect yourself to be perfect.

Relearning to Eat Instinctively

To resolve your weight and food issues without endless dieting you must restore your Instinctive Eating Cycle. Instead of focusing on what and how much food you should eat, the key is first understanding why you want to eat in the first place. This awareness will give you the opportunity to meet your true needs appropriately.

The first step, simple yet powerful, is to begin asking yourself "Am I hungry?" whenever you want to eat. This will help you recognize when the urge to eat is due to hunger and when it is due to some other trigger.

Furthermore, once you recognize which cycle you are in at any given moment, you can choose to re-enter the Instinctive Eating Cycle by asking yourself important questions at each Decision Point along the Eating Cycle. You will learn how to use each of these Decision Points to build the essential layers of lifetime weight management skills throughout the following chapters.

Reach and Maintain a Healthier Weight by Asking, "Am I Hungry?"

Imagine what it will be like when you re-establish physical hunger as your primary cue for eating and learn to satisfy your other needs in positive and constructive ways. In essence you will create new pathways, for eating and for living.

You won't be required to count calories, exchanges, fat grams, or points. You won't be told to eliminate your favorite "fattening" foods. You won't need to tolerate tasteless food substitutes. You won't have to avoid certain restaurants or "cheat" on your birthday. And you won't need an endless supply of willpower and self-control.

There won't be any more good or bad foods to worry about. You will discover that it is possible to balance eating for nourishment with eating for enjoyment. Eating will become pleasurable again, free from guilt and feelings of deprivation.

This time, you will learn to listen to your body's messages about when to eat, what kinds of food satisfy you, and how much food you need—without following a restrictive diet. You will gain the tools to manage your weight no matter where you are or what you are doing—celebrating the holidays, doing business over lunch, or relaxing on vacation.

Food will begin to serve its proper function in your life—to satisfy hunger. Once you learn to recognize and respond appropriately to hunger, you will begin to see what other needs eating has been fulfilling and perhaps what role your weight is playing in your life as well.

Once you are empowered to manage your eating by listening to your own instincts, you will feel empowered to take charge of other areas in your life as well. You will feel more self-motivated to make healthy nutrition and fitness choices when they come from within rather than from an external set of rules.

As you break away from the Over Eating and Restrictive Eating Cycles, the Fitness and Nutrition sections of each chapter will show you how activity improves your health, energy, and well-being, and how food and eating fuels your body, your mind, and your spirit.

Ultimately, you will develop constructive skills and effective coping mechanisms to meet your other needs. Step by step, you will learn a whole new system for losing weight and building optimal health. You will free yourself from your focus on food and weight and discover new tools and energy to lead a more fulfilling, balanced life.

Fitness: Boosting Your Metabolism

It is an undeniable fact: to lose weight, you must use more fuel than you consume. All weight-loss plans are just variations on how to accomplish this—including this one. The difference is that *Am I Hungry?* guides you toward meeting your true needs, including your body's needs. Over Eating and Restrictive Eating often do not meet your body's needs. Worse yet, they often have negative effects on your metabolism. Therefore, understanding what metabolism means and how it works is essential if you are going to break out of those cycles and make your metabolism work for you.

By understanding how your body functions and uses the food you eat, you can choose to help your body become more metabolically active. The best way to optimally support and increase your metabolism is to live an active lifestyle and exercise regularly, maintain and build your muscle, and eat an appropriate amount of food to fuel your cells.

Understanding Your Metabolism

The word metabolism is thrown around a lot these days. People often complain about having a slow or sluggish metabolism. Many products promise to "boost" your metabolism. But what is metabolism anyway? In a nutshell, metabolism simply refers to the amount of fuel or energy, measured in calories, that your body burns each day. When most people think of burning calories, images of treadmills and aerobics classes come to mind. However, you are burning calories right now just reading this book. In fact, how you live

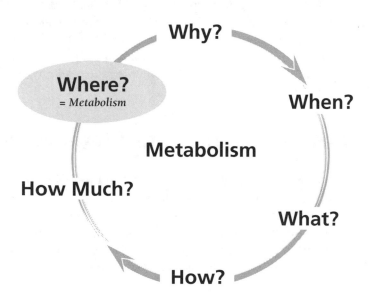

your life determines your metabolism—it is "Where" your energy goes.

Your Basal Metabolism

Think of your metabolism as the amount of fuel your body burns, represented here as a fuel can. The largest part, called basal metabolism, is the number of calories your body burns to support your basic bodily functions. These vital functions include your heartbeat, breathing, brain function, and numerous other important, but invisible, activities going on inside of you at all times. Even eating, digesting, and processing food contribute to your metabolism.

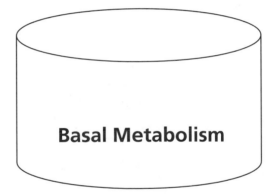

Basal Metabolism

In fact, every little cell in your body is like a tiny engine that burns fuel continuously in the process of doing its job. These tiny engines never shut off—at least while you are living. Even when you're sleeping or sitting still, your body's cells are still actively working just to keep you alive. It's just like your car; when the engine is running, it is burning fuel—even if it is just sitting in the driveway.

Activity Boosts Your Metabolism

Your activity level is another significant part of your fuel needs. On top of your basal metabolism, your body's workload increases with any type of activity, from brushing your teeth and taking a shower, to walking around your home or office. This extra work boosts the number of calories the cells burn, because the labor of the cells has increased. For instance, your lung cells must work to take in oxygen and release carbon dioxide, but they work harder when you're walking at a brisk pace than when you're sitting in a chair. The more you demand from your body, the more calories each tiny cell burns while doing its job.

Anything you do above your basal metabolic level constitutes activity. This includes lifestyle activities—all of the things that you do throughout your day-to-day existence. In fact, many of the people who seem to have a high metabolism are actually just more active throughout their day. A few added steps here and there, and a little extra effort during everyday work and play really add up.

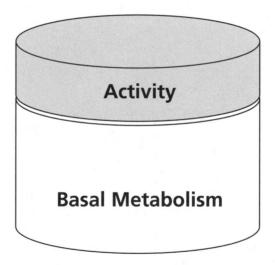

In addition to an active lifestyle, regular exercise is another great way to boost your physical activity level and therefore, your metabolism. Obviously, a person who walks two miles a day will burn more calories and will be more fit than someone who does not exercise at all. Exercise is a very effective metabolism booster. Not only does it burn more calories while you are doing it, it even raises the amount of fuel your cells burn for awhile afterward. The point is that any additional lifestyle activity or exercise above your basal rate will raise your metabolism.

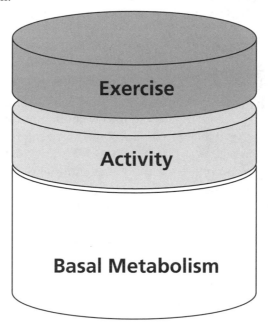

Muscle Burns Calories

Another piece to this metabolic puzzle is your body composition. Your body is composed of water, adipose tissue (better known as fat), and lean tissue, which is everything else (muscle, bone, hair, and other tissues). Muscle mass is part of your lean tissue and is a significant contributor to an active metabolism. A majority of your body's machinery is composed of muscle, including many of your internal organs. Muscles help you breathe, digest food, move your body, lift and carry objects, and even stand upright. The tiny engines of muscle cells burn more energy than less active cells. Therefore, muscle is metabolically active tissue because it requires a significant amount of energy to perform its work. Muscle cells burn more calories than fat cells because the workload, or demand, on muscles is so much greater.

Not only do muscle cells require more energy to do their work, but it also takes energy to maintain them. A pound of muscle burns more calories each day than a pound of fat. Muscles are maintained simply by using them regularly. However, whenever you do more than your body is accustomed to, your body will build more muscle to accommodate the new workload. Building this new muscle tissue requires even more fuel. Of course, once you build additional muscle tissue, it takes more energy to maintain it. In short, the more you increase the number of active cells that you have, the more calories you will burn. It's like a factory; as the number of workers increases, the productivity, or output, goes up. By maintaining the muscle you have and building new muscle tissue, you will burn more calories per day, boost your metabolic rate, and turn your body into an energy-burning machine.

Understanding your metabolism isn't difficult. More importantly, improving your metabolism isn't all that difficult either. You will learn how to boost your metabolism, improve your energy, reconnect with your body, and enhance your sense of well-being by increasing your exercise and lifestyle activity levels.

Nutrition: Fueling Your Metabolism

To help you begin to make the best possible choices to satisfy your body and your soul, the nutrition sections in each chapter will focus on building your understanding of fundamental nutrition principles and facts. This foundation of practical nutrition information will help you make meaningful long-term changes.

Let's start by understanding how food fuels your metabolism.

Food is Fuel

There is another important part of metabolism—food. Your fuel intake plays a vital role in keeping this process running smoothly. When you eat for reasons other than hunger, you will

take in more food than your body requires and create a surplus of fuel. This excess fuel is stored as body fat until it is needed later.

On the other hand, cells must have an energy supply in order to perform their required tasks. Without an adequate amount of fuel, your cells cannot function properly, resulting in some unfavorable consequences. Think about your car again. If it runs out of gasoline, it will putter and stop. However, because you must stay alive, your body's cells cannot all just shut off. When your cells are short on fuel from food, your body will turn to its reserve tanks to utilize other energy sources. Initially, it will use up carbohydrates that have been stored as glycogen in your muscles and liver. When that is gone, it will begin to break down certain tissues to use for its energy supply, specifically fat and muscle.

Conserving Energy

In a state of ongoing fuel shortage or semi-starvation, your body must pick and choose which cells to continue supporting and which ones to drop. A priority list is developed, and needless to say, the cells that provide vital activities take top priority. Remember, muscle cells require a lot of energy, so those that aren't being used regularly will be given the pink slip. This loss of calorie-burning muscle is a real blow to your metabolism.

When your food supply remains low, your cells must also become more efficient. That is, they attempt to perform their jobs without burning as many calories; they adapt to the lower energy intake by expending less energy. If this happened in your car, you'd be thrilled, but when it happens in your body, you're in trouble. Your body could be burning 20 percent to 36 percent fewer calories per day by becoming more fuel-efficient. Furthermore, after a period of energy deprivation, your body becomes more efficient at storing body fat because it is less metabolically active and fat provides a ready source of extra fuel. The result is that it is easier for you to gain weight, harder for you to lose weight, and you feel sluggish and weak.

Essentially your body is required to manage the difference between the number of calories you feed it and the number of calories it burns. When you take in too much fuel, your body will save it for later. When you take in far fewer calories than your body needs, your metabolism will eventually decrease. Your body is remarkably effective at managing your metabolism to prevent death by starvation.

Your Body is Programmed to Survive

While it seems that diets often backfire, this is simply the result of your body adapting to being under-fueled. Your body has primitive, complex survival mechanisms that help keep you alive during limited periods of starvation. In days long ago when food was not as plentiful or easy to obtain, people worked quite strenuously hunting and gathering their food. Perhaps they chased wild game or walked miles to find edible berries and roots. When they were able to eat freely, their bodies used the fuel as needed for activities and stored any extra fuel as fat for later use. When food supplies were scarce during cold winters or summer droughts, their bodies could draw on the stored fat for fuel.

If a famine persisted, their bodies would sense the lack of sufficient fuel and conserve energy by eliminating non-essential functions and slowing down the essential ones. Fat stores and muscle tissue would be broken down for energy to meet their bodies' caloric demands. When the famine was over and they could eat whenever they were hungry, their bodies would rebuild lost fuel stores. Their muscle mass would also be rebuilt as their tasks of hunting and gathering of food were supported by adequate nourishment.

Your body still has this primitive survival mechanism, but in many areas of modern society food is abundant and readily available. Generally speaking, most modern famines are the result of self-imposed starvation diets. Under strict dieting conditions, the same old survival mechanisms still exist. Initially you will lose water and some of your stored fuel. However, when your survival mechanisms kick in, your metabolism decreases to conserve energy, and some of your muscle mass may be lost. As a result, you burn fewer calories each day and your weight loss slows down. This is the frustrating plateau dieters so often experience.

When the diet is over and you return to your previous eating habits, your body quickly replaces its fat stores. Unless you are actively exercising, you will not rebuild the majority of the muscle tissue you lost during the diet.[1] Ultimately, this causes you to have a lower metabolic rate and a higher body fat percentage than before the diet. This explains the irony that most people end up less healthy than before they tried to lose weight by going on a diet.

So What Does Work?

At this point you may be thinking, "If diets don't work, what am I supposed to do?" You have been bombarded with information about eating right and exercising so you probably

---

1 An exception to this occurs when a person has lost essential muscle mass necessary for basic daily activities and bodily function as occurs in extended periods of starvation and anorexia nervosa. This essential muscle tissue will be rebuilt as soon as adequate nourishment is supplied.

know the fundamental principle of weight loss: the number of calories you eat must be less than the number of calories you burn. Yet, despite all of the information available on the countless ways to accomplish this, you and millions of others still battle with weight issues. Many people continue to try one diet after another, while others have simply given up.

It is time to face the fact that the key to solving your struggle with weight and food does not lie in a magical, or even logical, combination of diet and exercise. The real solution is in re-learning the use of innate and instinctive eating patterns and thereby eating in a way which fuels your metabolism. By finally addressing your relationship with food you can work toward optimal health rather than some arbitrary weight goal.

But first, you must give up on dieting. Forever! While that may be a relief, it may not be as easy as it sounds. Your diet thoughts and behaviors may have become so ingrained that you don't even recognize them for what they are. *Am I Hungry?* will help you let go of dieting and learn a way of achieving optimal health that is harmonious with the whole you.

Am I Hungry? will show you how your food choices can fuel your body, mind, and spirit. You will see that eating to satisfy hunger is pleasurable and that it is good to eat foods that you enjoy. You will find that meeting your other needs in appropriate ways will bring balance and joy to your life. You will learn to balance eating for nutrition with eating for enjoyment. You will develop the skills to enhance your enjoyment of food, your body, and your life.

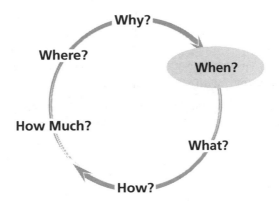

CHAPTER 2

Decision Point: Am I Hungry?

At this point you are beginning to understand some of the reasons why weight loss diets haven't worked for you (or most people). In the past you may have started diets to help you gain control over your eating, but now you recognize that diets usually just tell you *how* you should eat and don't really address *why* you are eating in the first place. The skills you will learn from *Am I Hungry?* will be very different. The goal is to lose your obsessions with food, dieting, and your weight, without giving you a long list of rules to follow. Although this book contains a lot of information about nutrition and healthy eating, it won't tell you when, what, and how much to eat. This should be a relief.

It may be scary too. You may be asking yourself, "If there aren't strict guidelines about food, won't I begin to eat uncontrollably? If an outside 'expert' doesn't tell me, how will I know what, when, and how much to eat? How will I know when to stop? How will I reach my healthy weight and stay there?"

This time, you will learn to become your own expert. After all, it's your body and your mind. Aren't you the best person to make decisions about how you should eat? Of course you will need information and new skills to make the best choices for yourself, but you already have the most important tool you'll need: hunger.

Hunger is your powerful internal guide that will help you reach and maintain your healthy weight. You may have ignored hunger for so long that you have forgotten how to recognize it. You may even blame it for your weight problem and see it as the enemy. However, by focusing on hunger as your guide, you will become your own internal authority for when, what, and how much to eat. You don't have to be in control, but you will learn to be in charge.

What is the Purpose of Hunger?

Human beings and other animals are born with a natural ability to regulate their dietary intake to meet their nutritional needs. Hunger and satiety are caused by complex biological pathways not yet fully understood. Simply put, hunger is your body's way of telling you that you need fuel.

Consider a newborn baby. Within hours, an infant begins to express her hunger by crying. When the baby is fed and her hunger is satisfied, her cries are soothed until the sensation of hunger returns and the cycle is repeated. Certainly a baby cries for many reasons, but if you try to feed her (instead of changing her, holding her, or warming her), the baby will spit out the nipple and turn away from the food. Soon, the attentive caretaker learns the meanings of the different cries and tries to satisfy them appropriately.

As the baby grows and begins to eat solid food, she lets you know when she has had enough by turning away from the spoon—or spitting the food back at you if you force the food in anyway. When she becomes a toddler, she seems to be in perpetual motion as she explores her new world. She barely stops long enough to eat a handful of crackers here and a few slices of banana there. The child never stops to ask the question,

"Am I hungry?" yet somehow manages to eat enough to grow and maintain a healthy weight.

Children instinctively respond to hunger, so their body trusts that it will be provided with the energy it needs for activity and survival. If food is readily available and eaten when the hunger signals come, the body will burn fuel freely as needed, resulting in an active metabolism. Further, children are too busy exploring and playing to bother thinking about food and eating, until hunger tells them to.

Unfortunately, over time many people have learned to ignore their own hunger signals. Perhaps you eat in response to external cues like meal times, advertisements, and the sight or smell of food. Others may have rewarded and comforted you with food, so you reward and comfort yourself the same way. Many social gatherings revolve around food and eating. People often express love and closeness by sharing food. You also learn to ignore hunger cues when you diet. You may actually feel proud of yourself when you don't allow yourself to eat even if you are physically hungry.

At the same time, you may have learned to ignore the feeling of satisfaction so you eat until you are overly full and uncomfortable. You may have learned to clean your plate, never waste food, and eat all your dinner if you want dessert, instead of stopping when you've had enough. And you will perpetuate the cycle by teaching your children the same things.

When you become disconnected from hunger and satiety, you lose the ability to regulate your intake to meet your body's needs. When you reconnect with these signals, you can reach and maintain a healthy weight without restrictive dieting.

Ironically, hunger can help you lose weight. You will eat less food when you are eating to satisfy physical hunger than if you eat to satisfy other needs. Think about it. If you are not hungry when you start eating, how do you know when to stop? Many people say that they stop when they are stuffed, when the food is gone, or when something interrupts their eating. Soon, you will learn to enjoy feeling comfortable at the end of a meal instead of feeling miserable. You will find it easier to stop when you are satisfied because you will know that you can eat again when hunger returns.

Besides, food just tastes better when you are truly hungry. When you wait until you are hungry, eating is more pleasurable and satisfying. In fact, the only way to be really satisfied with food is to eat because you are physically hungry. Once you have experienced the pleasure of eating when you are truly hungry, you will begin to relish the prospect of hunger arriving. Hunger is truly the best seasoning.

Am I Hungry?

With an understanding of the basic Eating Cycle from Chapter 1, you are now able to add another layer of information to guide your eating decisions.

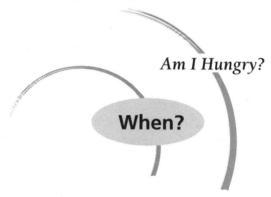

There is a remarkably simple but powerful way to learn to use hunger to guide your eating again. Whenever you want to eat, ask yourself, "Am I hungry?" This important question will help you recognize the difference between an urge to eat caused by the physical need for food, from an urge to eat caused by other triggers. This awareness will give you the opportunity to meet your true needs appropriately. In essence, you will create new pathways, not only for eating, but for living.

Am I hungry? When you ask yourself this question before you start eating, you will become your own authority on what you need. You will discover not only what your body's nutritional needs are, but you will begin to recognize when you are tempted to use food to meet other needs. To begin this process, you will need to know more about hunger.

What Does Hunger Feel Like?

It is very common for people who have struggled with food and their weight to be disconnected from the physical sensations of hunger. For many different reasons, they simply don't recognize or pay attention to the true symptoms of hunger.

Many people say they are hungry all of the time. However, it is unlikely that a person would be physically hungry constantly; wanting to eat is not the same thing as hunger. Many people misinterpret other physical symptoms and sensations like thirst, fatigue, or nervousness for hunger. Even more commonly, people confuse emotional or environmental triggers, cravings, and appetite with hunger.

Other people have told us that they are never hungry. Again, it is unlikely that a person would never be hungry. Sometimes, people miss the signals of hunger because they don't really know how hunger feels or they are too busy or distracted to notice. Sometimes they have learned to ignore hunger in order to control their weight. But most often, people who say they are never hungry really aren't. They feed themselves so frequently for other reasons that their body never really needs to tell them that they need more fuel.

Before reading ahead, stop and think for a moment. How do you know when you are hungry? What does it really feel like? Write down all of the signs that let you know when you are hungry.

Because people experience hunger in different ways, the following list of the most common hunger symptoms can help you identify your personal signs of hunger:

- Hunger pangs
- Growling or grumbling in the stomach
- Empty feeling
- Gnawing

- Slight queasy feeling
- Weakness or loss of energy
- Trouble concentrating
- Lightheadedness
- Slight headache
- Irritability or crankiness
- Feeling that you must eat as soon as possible

What Causes Hunger?

What causes symptoms of hunger? To really understand how hunger feels, it helps if you understand what causes it. Hunger symptoms are caused by a combination of your stomach's emptiness or fullness, your body's need for energy, and various hormones and other substances in your body. This is an exciting area of research currently, but from a practical standpoint we will focus on your stomach and blood sugar, since those cause the most recognizable and concrete symptoms.

Your stomach is composed of muscle-like tissue that squeezes food to break it apart, mixes it with digestive enzymes, and moves it into the intestines. When the stomach is empty, its muscular wall begins to contract causing the growling or rumbling you may feel or hear when you are hungry. This causes an empty feeling for some people. Since the stomach produces small amounts of digestive acids even when there is no food present, some people get sensations of gnawing or queasiness.

At the same time, you may notice symptoms of your blood sugar (called glucose) dropping. Your body primarily uses glucose from your bloodstream for energy. As your blood sugar falls, you may notice that your energy level begins to dip and it may be harder to concentrate. As you get hungrier, you may feel lightheaded or develop a headache.

Hunger can also trigger mood changes. Many people become irritable and cranky when they are hungry. They may become impatient or short-tempered. Unfortunately, a lot of people are not aware that hunger can cause them to act this way—but the people around them sure notice! It is especially helpful to observe these symptoms in hungry children and help them begin to recognize when they are hungry. It is much easier to change bad behavior by feeding a cranky, hungry child than trying to discipline them into good behavior.

As you become hungrier, the symptoms may become stronger until you reach a point when you feel that you absolutely must eat. If you wait any longer to supply your body with energy, you simply won't care what you eat, as long as you get something into your stomach. Waiting to eat until you are ravenous can lead to overeating.

What Happens When You Eat?

When you eat, your digestive system breaks down and absorbs the food, causing these hunger symptoms to subside. Food and fluids fill out the shape of the stomach, like filling a sack with sand. As you eat or drink more, the stomach becomes full and begins to stretch. As the stomach walls expand, you will begin to feel a sense of fullness. If you continue to eat, the stomach walls stretch further, and you may begin to feel discomfort or even pain. Depending on the location where you are dining, you may be tempted to loosen your belt or unbutton your skirt to make room for your expanding stomach.

When you eat, energy is drawn to the stomach and digestive system to break down the food. That is why your mother told you to wait thirty minutes after you ate to go swimming. When you eat a small amount of food, you will not even be aware that the digestive process is going on. However, if there are large amounts or very heavy foods to digest, you may notice that you feel drowsy and sluggish after eating. It may be difficult to be productive and concentrate when you are digesting a lot of food.

The type of food and how much you eat determines how long the digestive process takes. After the food is broken down for energy, your body can use the fuel for its activities. It will store any extra fuel in the form of body fat until it is needed.

When the stomach is empty and the fuel is gone, the entire hunger cycle repeats itself.

Strategies For Identifying Hunger

When you learn something new, or in this case, re-learn something you have forgotten, it helps to have a strategy. Throughout this book there are specific strategies to help you learn new skills to reach and maintain your healthy weight without dieting. These strategies should not be read and set aside. Instead, they must be practiced over and over, like riding a bike, until they are mastered. With practice, the skills will become automatic so you won't even have to think about them anymore. This process of learning new strategies will help you become an instinctive eater again.

Some of the sensations of hunger are subtle and can be easily missed if you are not accustomed to noticing them. To identify hunger, you need to know what to look for and how to find them. To recognize the symptoms of hunger, try these strategies.

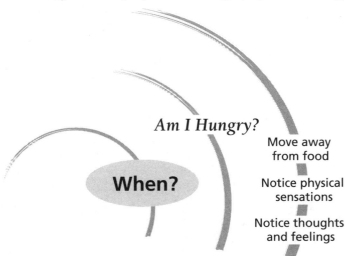

Am I Hungry?

When?

Move away from food

Notice physical sensations

Notice thoughts and feelings

- First, remove yourself from the sight and smell of food. The presence of food may trigger the desire to eat and confuse you when you are trying to decide if you are truly hungry. To minimize mixed signals, try to move away

from any location or situation that you associate with
eating. This may include the kitchen, dining room, break
room, or even the living room, bedroom, or car if you are
in the habit of eating in those locations. One woman said
that the bathroom is the best place for her to figure out if
she is really hungry because there is nothing in there that
triggers her desire to eat. If you are planning to eat at a
restaurant, determine how hungry you are before you get
out of the car. At a party, you can step outside and admire
the backyard for a moment in order to tune into your
signals.

- Tune out the environment. Once you are away from food
  and any food associations, close your eyes for a moment.
  If you can't get away from the food or situation, try to
  tune out your surroundings for a few moments.

- Take a few deep breaths and calm yourself. Be aware that
  being near food or thinking about eating might cause you
  to feel excited or anxious, making it more difficult to
  identify the signs of hunger. By taking a few calming
  breaths first, it will be easier to focus on important
  sensations and feelings.

- Connect with your sensations. Since hunger is a physical
  sensation, connect with your body by placing your hand
  on your upper abdomen, just below your ribcage. Picture
  your stomach. Think of it like a balloon or a rubber sack.
  Try to imagine how full the balloon or sack is. Your
  stomach is about the size of your loosely clenched fist
  when it is empty and can stretch several times that size
  when it is full.

- Ask yourself, "Am I hungry?" What physical sensations
  can you identify? Are there pangs, growling, rumbling, or
  gnawing sensations? Does your stomach feel empty, full,
  or even stuffed? Perhaps you are neither hungry nor full
  and can't feel your stomach at all.

- Notice other physical signals. Do you feel edgy,
  lightheaded, or weak? Are these signals coming from
  hunger, or from something else? Tune into your body. Are

you thirsty, tired, or anxious? This is a great opportunity to start reconnecting with your inner self.

- Notice what you are thinking. Quite often, your thoughts will give you clues about whether or not you are hungry. If you find yourself rationalizing or justifying, "It's been four hours since I last ate; I should be hungry," you may be looking for an excuse to eat. If you have any doubts about whether you are physically hungry, you probably aren't.

- Let go of negative thoughts. Become aware of any negative thoughts that you are having about eating. Keep in mind that hunger is a normal sensation and eating is the best way to satisfy it. There is no need to feel guilty about this natural process.

What Isn't Hunger?

People sometimes have difficulty distinguishing between true physical hunger and the other physical sensations, feelings, and thoughts that may be confused with hunger. Let's look at those briefly.

Thirst: Surprisingly, many people think they are hungry when they are thirsty. We get a lot of fluid from the food we eat, but that is a very inefficient way of taking care of thirst. You might try drinking a large glass of water to see if that satisfies your symptoms of hunger before you begin to eat food that your body doesn't really need.

Fatigue: Feeling a lack of energy can be a sign of hunger when your blood sugar drops, but a low energy level can also be due to mental or physical fatigue. Eating will only help your energy level if you need calories; eating won't really help if you need a nap. It is important to meet your body's need for rest and sleep in order to feel your best. In fact, eating when you are not hungry only makes you feel more tired because your body has to work to digest and process the unneeded food.

Salivation: Salivating is a normal physical response to the sight, the smell, or even the thought of appetizing food. Saliva contains small amounts of digestive enzymes so it can begin the digestive process while you are chewing. Since salivation occurs with or without hunger, it is not a reliable sign that your body needs food.

Environmental triggers: External cues, like mealtimes or social gatherings, may also trigger an urge to eat. A famous scientist, Ivan Pavlov, measured the saliva that dogs produced when eating. He then rang a bell every time he fed the dogs. After a period of time, he found that the dogs would salivate whenever he rang the bell—even if he didn't feed them. Environmental triggers are similar to Pavlov's bell. If you are used to eating in certain situations and at certain times, you may confuse the association with true hunger. Paying attention to physical symptoms of hunger, like feeling your stomach growl, will help you recognize the difference.

Urge to eat: Thoughts of food and eating may signal that you are becoming hungry. However, you can think about food and eating for many other reasons. Try not to fool yourself into thinking you are hungry just because you want to eat! Again, you must look for some of the other physical symptoms too.

Cravings: Cravings can be another challenging area. Although you may have cravings for specific foods when you are hungry, having cravings doesn't mean that you are hungry. If you find yourself searching through the refrigerator or the pantry, walking back to the break room at work, or peering into a snack machine to find something to satisfy a taste craving, you may try to convince yourself that you are hungry. You can change this habit by simply stopping long enough to ask yourself the question, "Am I hungry?"

Boredom: Boredom is not hunger. Eating will certainly give you something to do when you are bored (or help you put off doing something you don't really want to do), but be careful. Do not try to convince yourself that you are hungry to justify eating.

Tension: Physical sensations that may be confused with hunger are nervousness, anxiety, or tension. It makes sense when you think about it. Butterflies in the stomach can feel a little bit like growling if you are not consciously aware that you are nervous. In fact, eating may even temporarily ease that sensation—but that still doesn't mean you are hungry. Besides, there are other ways of managing those feelings that will make you feel better without gaining weight. When you think you might be hungry, just ask yourself if you could be nervous, anxious, or tense.

Urge to chew, crunch, or suck: A desire to chew, crunch, or suck are physical urges that can be triggered by certain emotions. But that does not mean your body needs the food that you want to chew, crunch, or suck on. If the urge is strong, look for non-caloric ways to satisfy it such as chewing gum and ice or sucking on calorie-free candies. Of course, using tobacco is not a healthy way to satisfy this urge.

Emotional triggers: Many emotions such as sadness, anger, loneliness, or frustration can trigger the urge to eat. Since you may have learned to soothe discomfort or distract yourself from certain feelings by eating, these feelings can make you think you are hungry. There is a great deal more to explore about emotional triggers but for now, try to increase your awareness of these connections when you are deciding whether or not you are hungry.

You will have many opportunities to practice identifying hunger since the urge to eat may occur many times each day. With time and practice, recognizing hunger and using it to guide your eating will become natural and instinctive again.

Fitness: Build a Positive Attitude Toward Exercise

Most people know that physical activity is very important, yet many people choose to lead sedentary lives—and even more find it difficult to start an exercise program or stick with it. On the other hand, some people use exercise merely for weight control and don't recognize how critical it is for achieving optimal health.

Although exercise is one of the most powerful tools available for improving health and managing weight, even the word exercise can conjure up negative thoughts and feelings. If you are not very active or not exercising regularly, perhaps you have some negative thoughts of your own. Take a look at some of the thoughts other people have about exercise and how we helped them think about it in more positive ways.

"I know I should exercise but I hate it so I just can't seem to make myself do it." Many people have negative feelings about exercise, as can be heard by the use of words like "should," "hate," and "make myself." These thoughts and feelings come from negative past experiences like being chosen last for teams, boring exercise routines, and discomfort or pain from doing too much, too fast. Some people only exercise when they are trying to lose weight so they have come to think of exercise as a punishment for their overeating.

However, the past does not predict the future. This time you can find fun physical activities that suit your personality and lifestyle. You can start slowly and allow your body to adjust gradually so it is not uncomfortable. You can choose to focus on all the great things it does for you and how wonderful you feel instead of how much weight you should lose. It can be different this time if you believe it will be.

"I don't know if exercise is really worth the effort." Actually, research has shown that exercise does make a difference. Studies have shown that 91 percent of people who lose weight and keep it off, exercise on a regular basis. By increasing your daily physical activity and exercising regularly, you will increase the number of calories you burn and improve your metabolism.

Even more importantly, exercise has many other well-documented health and psychological benefits. Among these are that it lowers blood pressure and blood sugar levels, improves cholesterol and energy levels, enhances mood and the sense of well-being, and helps you live longer. If you could buy all of that in a pill, everyone would want a prescription.

Exercise will also help you reconnect with your physical body. This is important since many people who struggle with their weight have disconnected with themselves from the neck down and feel that their body has betrayed them. Becoming more active will help you see that your body does serve you well and that it is capable of becoming more fit when you challenge it even a little. There is great joy to be found in simply moving your body. You see, exercise is not a means to an end, but an end in and of itself.

"I don't have time." It will only take 1/48th of your whole day to exercise for 30 minutes—and most people waste a lot more time than that on unproductive activities like watching TV. You probably make time for other grooming routines like bathing, putting on make-up, and washing your clothes, so you can make time for the increased activity. Exercise will do even more for your appearance, not to mention all of the psychological and health benefits you will gain. Being physically active is more important for your health and well-being than most of the other things you think must get done each day. Furthermore, studies have shown that two fifteen-minute sessions of exercise are just as beneficial as one thirty-minute session. The key to doing it is giving it the priority that it deserves.

"I don't have the energy." No matter how you feel initially, you are likely to find that you feel better within just a few minutes of starting to exercise. These good feelings usually last long after the exercise is finished, too. Have you ever noticed that fit people seem to have more energy than others? It turns out that exercise increases your strength and stamina, and helps you sleep better so you will become more productive and feel great. So even when you feel tired, commit to exercising for at least ten minutes. Promise yourself that you can stop and try again another day if you still aren't feeling any better. Most of the time you will feel so good that you will want to continue.

"I'll start exercising when I've lost some of this weight." Doing any kind of extra physical activity uses additional calories and makes it easier to lose weight in the first place. In addition, physical activity reduces cravings and curbs your appetite by raising your endorphins (feel-good chemicals) and serotonin levels (calm chemicals). Besides, if you don't exercise while you are losing weight, you may lose fat *and* muscle. It may become

gradually harder to lose weight—and almost impossible to keep it off. But cardiorespiratory exercise and weight training will minimize your loss of lean body mass during weight loss.

"I'm embarrassed to be seen exercising." Ironically most other people are so focused on themselves, they are not going to notice you anyway. Those that do will likely admire you. Eventually you will feel less self-conscious, but in the meantime, find activities and places that make you feel comfortable so you can focus on all of the wonderful benefits. Remember, you are doing this for yourself—to feel better and become healthier.

"Exercise is really hard for me." Physical activity doesn't have to be hard or hurt to be beneficial. In fact, it is more important to find an activity that is convenient, comfortable, and enjoyable so you'll stick with it. Finding a partner, trying new activities and new routes, rewarding yourself with a hot bath or massage, and setting small, achievable goals are great ways to make exercise more fun. Even if you have physical limitations it is always possible to find some way to increase your activity level. If you have been very inactive, start by increasing your lifestyle activity then work toward a regular exercise routine. You will be amazed at how much your body can adapt to whatever challenges you give it.

"I'm so out of shape—I don't even know where to start!" Of course it is important to check with your doctor before you begin any new exercise program. Once you have been medically cleared, you have to start somewhere—so start where you are. There is no such thing as instant fitness. If you start this week by increasing your activity level, little by little, three months from now you will be leaner, stronger, more energetic, and healthier. If you choose not to start, then don't be surprised if you are exactly the same as you are today.

"I can't do what they recommend so why bother?" Get rid of the notion that you have to exercise for 30-45 minutes, 4-5 days a week, or not at all. That is ridiculous! Increased activity throughout the day really adds up. Simply taking the stairs, walking a little faster, and working or playing a little harder everyday can accomplish this. Any activity over your usual level counts, so be on the look out for opportunities to "just do it!"

"I have a strenuous job so I don't need to exercise when I get home." Your activity at work and at home definitely contributes to your overall level of fitness but few jobs provide all of the elements of a great fitness program.

"I was doing pretty well until I got sick (or busy, or company came, or I went on vacation ...)." Quitting your exercise program because you missed a day, a week, or even longer makes as much sense as eating the whole bag of cookies because you ate three. No person and no schedule are ever perfect. If this is going to become part of your life, you need to be as consistent but as flexible as possible. Many people have found that writing their exercise schedules on their calendars helps them stay on track. If they miss a session, they simply reschedule it, the way they would any other important appointment.

"I started exercising but I quit because I wasn't seeing the weight loss I expected." Fitness is a process that takes time. Whether you are losing weight or not, you are becoming healthier. When you focus only on weight loss, you lose sight of the most important goal—building optimal health. Instead, set realistic goals and watch for the many other benefits of exercise like having the stamina to play with your grandchildren and not feeling winded just walking to the mailbox.

"I already exercise but I am still overweight." Chances are, you would weigh more if you didn't exercise. Don't forget that the real purpose of exercise is to become healthier and feel better so keep in mind that overweight people who exercise are healthier than "ideal" weight individuals who are inactive. Studies have also shown that exercise alone is not as effective for weight loss as is exercise plus a reduction in caloric intake. Since weight loss requires that you consume fewer calories than you use, learning to eat according to your hunger cues is a very important part of this process. We have also found that some people get stuck in the exercise rut of doing the same thing all of the time so they aren't getting as much out of their exercise as they could. Instead, try new types of activities, and increase the amount of time, frequency, and intensity of your exercise. This keeps your body challenged and your exercise plan from becoming boring.

What are your other negative thoughts and attitudes about exercise? Can you counter them in a positive way? Develop positive statements about activity and repeat them often to yourself. For instance, instead of saying, "Exercise is boring," say, "Being active gives me the opportunity to relieve stress and feel better." Repeat affirmations like, "I can feel myself becoming healthier and more energetic." "It feels so good to move my muscles." and "I can do it!" Repeat these positive statements frequently. This way you will begin to undo your negative feelings whenever you find yourself slipping into those old thought patterns that prevented you from becoming more physically active in the past. Start thinking of yourself as an active, healthy person—and you will become one.

Nutrition: All Foods Fit

You have already learned your most important guide: whenever you want to eat, ask yourself, "Am I hungry?" Once you let go of all of those other restrictive and complicated diet rules and build a solid foundation of nutrition information you will be in charge of making the best possible choices for yourself. The nutrition sections in this book will provide you with the facts you need to create a nutrition plan that will help you build optimal health free from dieting. But giving up dieting is not always as easy as it sounds.

We live in a society that has become obsessed with weight and dieting. We are constantly bombarded with the latest weight loss scheme to "rid ourselves of those unsightly pounds." New fad diets scream at us from magazines and books, talk shows and news programs, commercials and testimonials, doctors' offices and health food stores. Americans spend billions of dollars annually on weight-loss products and services. Paradoxically, the more we diet, the heavier we become as a nation.

Medical research has proven that even a 5 percent weight loss can significantly improve health. With a 5 percent to 10 percent weight loss, you can reduce your risk of high blood pressure, diabetes, high cholesterol, heart disease, and some types of cancers. Of course, many people diet to look better. There is nothing wrong with losing weight to improve physical appearance and self-esteem, but many people have unrealistic expectations that drive them to lose weight—no matter the cost.

No matter what your motivation, the striking reality is that diets are not very effective in the long run. Accurate statistics are very hard to come by but it is widely quoted that 90 percent to 95 percent of dieters regain their lost weight. This is a difficult number to pin down since there are so many ways of losing weight, so many people trying it on their own, so few people studied for long periods of time, and so many people going off their diets before they lose a significant amount of weight in the first place. Whatever the numbers, if dieting was truly effective, your problem would have been solved with the first one.

Diets Are Just Rules

The diet message is loud and clear, "You are out of control so you need to follow our rules." The latest "expert" or authority may recommend counting calories, exchanges, points, grams, or ounces. The diet may require that you eat pre-packaged food or meal replacements. There may be strict meal plans or complicated diets to follow. Some methods eliminate entire food groups—or solid food all together. Diets may claim that there are magical food combinations or that some foods should be forbidden. And of course, the rules are changing all the time. No wonder so many people feel confused.

Most diets impose food rules that people do not, cannot, or should not follow for very long. When they can't stick to the rules, some dieters will resort to appetite suppressants to help control their hunger or dangerous thermogenics to boost their metabolism. Some people finally opt for drastic stomach bypass surgery to force changes in their eating.

Diets Require a Lot of Energy

Planning ahead and preparing healthy meals are important for a healthy diet, but dieting takes this to the extreme. Since diets are based on rules, you have to learn and follow the rules indefinitely for the diet to be effective. You may wake up in the morning thinking about food in order to plan what you will eat for the entire day—before you are even out of bed! You may find yourself counting out pretzel sticks, weighing chicken breasts, and measuring milk to make sure you are complying with the rules. You may carefully scrutinize every food label for calorie counts and forbidden ingredients. You may even avoid parties and your favorite restaurants so you are not tempted by the sinful pleasures you will find there.

The irony is that overeating was the reason you started the diet in the first place—but now all you think about is food. Ultimately this constant effort and vigilance may wear you out and cause you to return to your Over Eating Cycle to escape.

Diets Can Lead to Cravings

Most diets are based on limiting various foods in one way or another. This leads you to place certain foods on a pedestal, out of reach. At the beginning of a diet, you may feel happy to have this control over your eating.

However, when foods are forbidden, you start to place special value on them. In this way, food gains even more power over you.

When certain foods are restricted, you may begin to feel deprived. These feelings of deprivation can cause strong cravings. Remember how you craved rich, creamy peanut butter when you weren't supposed to eat fat, or piping hot bread when you were on a low-carbohydrate diet?

When you finally give in to the powerful cravings for these "bad" foods, you may feel guilty and out of control. You may give up the diet and even binge on the foods you've been missing. Of course, most dieters blame themselves when the diet fails, but in reality, dieting itself is to blame.

Diets Are Often Negative

Like most people, you probably become frustrated at how hard it is to stick to the diet's rules in the long run. After a while you start to feel deprived. But when you break the rules, you feel guilty. Due to this constant struggle, dieting often leads to a painful relationship with food.

Of course the other problem is that diets don't really address the reasons most people overeat in the first place. Although substituting celery sticks for potato chips may temporarily decrease your calories, if you are eating potato chips because you are bored, celery sticks aren't going to fill the bill either. So when the diet is over (and it will be, sooner or later), you will return to your previous eating habits. You end up having negative feelings about yourself because you believe that you have failed.

Some people manage to stick with the rules but they may become restrictive eaters in the process. They have to become experts at ignoring hunger and depriving themselves of foods they enjoy in order to stay in control—and control their weight. This is a significant price to pay since it takes a great deal of energy to eat only "good" foods and avoid the "bad" ones. With restrictive eating, eating often leads to conflict and guilt, not pleasure.

For all these reasons and others, dieting usually just leads to pain and disappointment. Since it is a proven concept that people do more of what brings them pleasure and strive to avoid what brings them pain, it is not surprising that diets are not an effective long-term solution to weight management.

Diets Are an External Authority

According to a growing anti-diet or non-diet movement, diets don't work because they are an external authority that teaches the dieter to disregard their own internal authority. Some diets don't let you eat even if you are hungry ("You are allowed to eat only 1400 calories per day.") or make you eat when you are not ("eat six small meals each day."). Diet messages tell you that you must learn to control yourself, and control your appetite, in order to gain control over your weight. You must follow the latest expert's rules about when, what, and how much to eat.

The end result is that dieting may separate you from your own body's cues of hunger and satiety. Therefore, you may move even further from your ability to know what your body really needs. Diets don't teach you about the importance of hunger as a natural guide for when, what, and how much food your body needs. When you diet, you have to be in *control*—but you are not *in charge* of your own eating.

"Good" Food, "Bad" Food

Fueling your body is the natural response to hunger. However, when you are trying to lose weight, you may experience conflict between what comes naturally, and what you think you are supposed to do. When you stand in front of your open refrigerator at home, what goes through your mind? "I shouldn't eat that; it is too fattening." "Hmmm. I wonder how many carbs that has?" "I guess I should eat this because it is healthy, but I really want something else." "Boy, I wish I was allowed to eat that."

This "good" food, "bad" food approach is common and may be contributing to your struggle with eating and weight. To make matters worse, many people feel confused about what they are supposed to eat since the rules seem to change frequently. People label foods to help them make healthier choices, but it takes a lot of effort to avoid all of the "bad" foods and consume only the "good" ones.

The truth is that all foods contain various quantities of nutrients and calories that are required for daily living. Some foods are more nutritionally beneficial than others—but that doesn't justify labeling them as "good" or "bad." That kind of black and white thinking does not free you from Over Eating and it doesn't move you any closer to optimal health.

All Foods Fit

The fact is, all foods fit. Think about people who eat instinctively. One distinguishing feature is that they eat whatever they want—when they are hungry. They don't obsess or worry about food. They may choose certain foods because they have learned about their health benefits, but they don't deprive themselves of foods that they find pleasurable. As a result, they are less likely to overeat their fun foods since they know they can have them anytime they want.

At this point, you may feel that if you let go of all the diet rules, you will only crave the diet's forbidden foods. That may happen at first, but as you transform yourself back into an instinctive eater and certain foods are no longer forbidden, your cravings for them will diminish. So, when you are hungry, instead of turning to a long list of restricted and allowed foods, keep in mind that all foods fit!

As you begin working through your food cravings and enjoying your favorite foods again, there are three simple but essential principles for effectively implementing the all foods fit approach: Balance, Variety, and Moderation.

Ken's experience provides us with a good example of why these are important:

> *When Ken worked as a technician, he brought his lunch to work most of the time. Then he got a new job in sales and his position became more stressful, with a lot of business entertaining and meetings over lunch. His diet shifted to large portion, high fat restaurant meals and as a result, he gained twenty pounds in his first year of the new job. He decided to try a high-protein, low-carbohydrate diet. It was easy at first since he could eat as much steak, bacon and eggs as he liked and he lost twelve pounds. However, he started missing many of the foods that were no longer allowed in his diet like pasta and fruit. He knew that some of those foods had been a source of pleasure for him and some were important for his health. He eventually found that he couldn't—and probably shouldn't, keep*

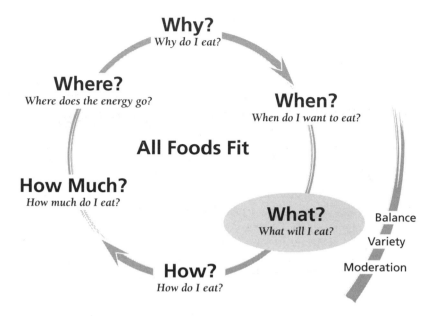

himself from eating all of those foods. Unfortunately, when he went back to his previous eating habits he regained all of the weight he had lost.

Principle One: Balance

Balance refers to the importance of providing your body with all of its necessary nutrients. But as Ken's experience shows, balance also refers to balancing eating for nourishment with eating for enjoyment. Whether he was on or off his diet, Ken was out of balance in both respects.

Principle Two: Variety

Variety refers to eating an assortment of different foods. As Ken discovered, eating the same foods all of the time leads to monotony. This was not only boring, but it did not meet all of his nutritional requirements. In fact, it is important not only to eat from all of the different food groups, but also to eat a mixture of foods within each group since no single food has everything you need. Variety in eating promotes overall health and enjoyment.

Principle Three: Moderation

Moderation refers to portion sizes but should not be confused with weighing and measuring food. These extreme methods are not necessary. The best way to determine if you have had enough is to listen to your cues of hunger and satiety. Many people don't listen to these cues even when they are dieting. They continue to overeat the foods that are allowed on their diet, so when the diet is over, they are still overeaters, just as Ken was. However, when your goal is to feel comfortable after eating, you are more likely to eat in moderation.

As you can see, this system does not rely on willpower, or more accurately *won't-power.* However, it does require increased awareness, basic knowledge, and new skills. When all foods fit and you use the principles of balance, variety, and moderation to guide you, the food you eat can help you build optimal health free from dieting.

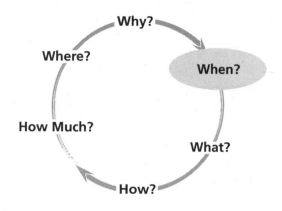

CHAPTER 3

Decision Point: I'm Not Hungry. What Are My Choices?

Now that you have re-learned to properly identify hunger, are you surprised how often you have an urge to eat without any physical indication that your body needs food?

You are in charge of what you do next. Notice how that is different from being in control. Being in control implies that you do things even when you don't want to or that you don't let yourself do things that you want to do. Control is what you need to follow the rules of a diet. Being in charge means that you get to make choices.

When you want to eat but you aren't hungry, you will get to make a choice. Remember, we said there is only one "rule" in this system: whenever you have an urge to eat, ask yourself, "Am I hungry?" We did not say, "You can only eat when you are hungry" or "If you are not hungry, you are not allowed to eat." If we did, this would be no different from any other diet that gives you rules to restrict your calorie intake.

The layers in this system were deliberately designed and tested to empower you to learn to make the best decisions for yourself, based on what works best for you in a given situation. This book is full of solid information and useful tools but ultimately, the decisions have to come from within you or the results will not be sustainable.

When I Want to Eat But I am Not Hungry, What Are My Choices?

If you want to eat but you aren't hungry, you have three choices: eat anyway, distract yourself, or become aware of what triggered the urge and address that need instead of eating. Each choice is valid and each choice has its advantages and disadvantages.

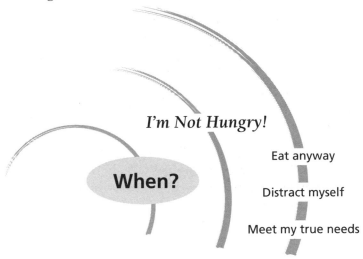

I'm Not Hungry!

When?

Eat anyway

Distract myself

Meet my true needs

Choice One: Eat Anyway

There are two main advantages to choosing to eat or choosing to keep eating even when you aren't hungry. First, it is usually the easiest thing to do so it doesn't require any thought or effort. Second, it may give you temporary satisfaction or pleasure. The key words are "may" and "temporary." You might be thinking to yourself, "But I always enjoy eating." However the truth is, most of the time it is just a habit carried out without any real awareness of the experience.

In reality, eating or continuing to eat when you aren't hungry often leads to the discomfort of fullness, then feeling sluggish and regretful afterward. And of course, one of the primary disadvantages is that when you eat food your body didn't ask for, it has no choice but to store it. Marla shares an example:

> *Almost every day after lunch I put my toddler down for a nap and turn on the television for a little break. There is usually nothing good on so I will watch the shopping channel or one of the cooking shows. I always want a snack so I will poke around in the cupboard until I find some crackers or cookies. Sometimes I even eat chocolate chips right out of the bag! I don't know why, but I'll find myself rummaging around in the refrigerator, munching on some cheese or grapes or even the leftovers from dinner. This can go on for an hour or more until I am just stuffed or my toddler wakes up. I get so mad at myself because I know that if I keep this up, I'll never be able to lose this weight. I always promise myself that I won't do it again tomorrow, but I usually do.*

Remember, even people who eat instinctively sometimes choose to eat (or overeat) even when they aren't particularly hungry—perhaps because of a special occasion or because the food looks or tastes wonderful. The point is that it is a choice. The difference is that the majority of the time instinctive eaters only eat when they are hungry.

If you choose to eat without hunger too often, you will struggle with your weight. We explained to Marla that being mad at herself wasn't really helping. Instead, she could begin to make a different choice.

Choice Two: Distract Yourself

Finding something else to do until the urge to eat passes is often an effective short-term strategy. When you give your mind something else to do and distract yourself from the food or the trigger, the urge to eat will pass within a few minutes. Marla tried it:

> *The day after we talked about trying to distract myself, I was in the same boat, wanting to snack while I watched T.V. after lunch. I knew I wasn't hungry so I decided to pay my bills instead of eating. It didn't help at all. But I wasn't ready to give up yet so I called my friend Jean and we talked for over half an hour. Before I knew it, my son was awake. We went to the park to play and by the time we got back, we were both hungry so we had a snack together. I felt great! For the rest of the week, whenever I started watching T.V. and got an urge to eat I called a different friend. It really worked—but I am running out of friends to call!*

Sometimes distraction is as simple as moving a candy dish out of sight or knitting instead of munching while you watch television. Distracting activities can be more involved, like working on a scrapbook page for a few hours or calling a friend to go for a walk. Here are a few strategies for choosing effective distractions:

- Make a list of activities that appeal to you *before* you need them. Write down both simple and more complicated ideas and be sure to include a few that don't require any preparation or equipment. You may have different ideas for home, work, and other settings. Add new activities to your list as you think of them. Having a variety of ideas ensures that you will come up with something that fits your mood or the situation.

- Chose activities that are enjoyable—or at least not unpleasant. If you are going to make a choice not to eat, the alternative must be somewhat appealing. Now you know why it didn't help Marla to try to pay her bills.

- If possible, choose an eating incompatible activity—any activity that requires your hands or full attention. For example, it is difficult to eat while you are playing the piano, building something, or sewing.

- Be prepared. Choose a few of the distractions from your list and have everything you need ready to go. For instance, if you plan to play a game of solitaire, keep the cards nearby. If you are going to try meditation, do a little reading about it ahead of time so you know what to do. You may want to make up a little distraction kit or keep an area in your home or office stocked with things to do—stationery, a favorite book, puzzles, tools, crafts, or anything else that appeals to you.

• When you want to eat but you aren't hungry, promise yourself that you will give one of your distractions a try, even if it is just for a little while. Remember that although it is easier to eat, when you make that choice, you will stay trapped in an Over Eating Cycle.

• Remember that you are distracting yourself because you are not hungry, not because you are depriving yourself. Tell yourself that you will eat when you are hungry.

Distracting yourself from eating works best when something in your environment triggered your urge to eat, like the sight of food. For Marla, watching cooking shows may have been triggering her afternoon binges. Like many people, she probably also associated relaxing and watching television with snacking. Getting away from the television was a good idea.

Distraction is very effective when the trigger to eat is boredom, the need for a break, or avoidance of another activity. In these situations, eating is certainly something to do—but there are many other options.

Distraction can also be helpful when you don't have the time or energy to figure out what the trigger was or how to deal with it right at that moment. However, the disadvantage of choosing to distract yourself is that when you don't address the underlying trigger, it will continue to result in the urge to eat, again and again. Which brings us to your third option.

Option Three: Become Aware

This is the most challenging option—but it is the most satisfying and can lead to the best long-term results. Choosing to become aware means figuring out where the urge to eat came from and dealing with that trigger. We explained this choice to Marla and here is what happened:

> *Getting away from the T.V. and calling a friend really helped me at first, but each day it was the same thing; I still had the urge to eat. After a week, I knew it was time to dig a little deeper. The next time it happened, I got up from the couch and went to my computer and just started typing my thoughts. It was amazing—here is part of it so you can see.*
>
> *"Here I am sitting in front of the computer because when I sit in front of the T.V. after Josh goes down I could eat myself out of house and home. I know it's worse when I watch cooking shows—all that great food and stuff. But it even happens when I am watching the shopping shows. One minute I am thinking about some new gadget or piece of jewelry that I want, and the next minute I want food. But it is not just stuff I want, I want something exciting to happen. I love being Josh's mommy but I loved working too. I kind of feel like my life is on hold and I am losing part of who I am."*

We have a saying, "When a craving doesn't come from hunger, eating will never satisfy it." Marla's story demonstrates this well. Her cravings weren't coming from a need for food—after all she just finished lunch—so no matter how much she ate, she didn't feel satisfied. Getting away from the T.V. and calling her friends was helpful. Not only did it distract her but it also gave her a connection with other people. Ultimately however, the most effective choice for her was to become aware of what was really triggering her urge to eat.

The source of your triggers may not always be dramatic or profound. Many triggers are simply learned habits like eating popcorn at the movies. In fact, triggers can be just about anything—physical, environmental, or emotional. Further, it is important to understand that most people who struggle with food and their weight do not have major underlying psychological problems. Eating to deal with certain emotions is simply a way of coping. However, if you realize that you have difficult emotions or issues to address, it is very important to seek out professional assistance from a doctor, counselor, therapist, or some other trained and supportive person.

In Marla's case, she had been handling the transition of being a stay-at-home mother by watching T.V. and eating. Eating is not the most effective way for you to cope but there is certainly no need to feel guilty or ashamed. At least you have been coping in some way. This is your opportunity to choose a more effective way.

Now What?

Once she recognized what the trigger was, Marla was able to choose to fulfill her real needs.

> *When I read what I wrote back to myself I cried. I thought about it for a few days then I decided to start taking some online classes so I can finish up my degree. I am so energized! I don't even want to watch T.V. now— much less eat all afternoon.*

Once you are aware of your triggers, you have an opportunity to meet those needs in a more productive way. That may be as simple as screaming into a pillow to cope with frustration or allowing yourself to read for awhile as a reward for working hard all day.

Sometimes the underlying need is much larger and will require time and additional tools to manage. Even then, it helps to take a small, positive action toward addressing that need. For instance, if you feel you really need a vacation, planning your trip is a step in the right direction.

Once you can distinguish between the *desire to eat* and *hunger*, you can decide what you will choose to do. It is not necessary to make a perfect choice every time in order to break free from your Over Eating and Restrictive Eating Cycles. It is simply a matter of becoming aware, recognizing that you have choices, and taking steps toward meeting your true needs. You won't have to *control* your eating because you will be in *charge* of your life.

Fitness: Live a More Active Lifestyle

Modern society has developed ways to do almost everything more efficiently, automatically, and effortlessly. While these conveniences may save time, they also save energy—your energy, which may result in increased weight. Even more significantly, a low level of lifestyle activity results in decreased fitness so you may not have the stamina, strength, or flexibility to live your life to the fullest.

Take stock of your own lifestyle. Are you active or sedentary? Do you avoid doing things that require effort? Would you like to feel more fit? Are you able to do all of the things you would like?

If you have been very inactive, any additional movement is a positive step toward a more active lifestyle. A simple walk to the mailbox or a short stroll during your lunch hour will get you started. You will be amazed at how quickly your body adapts to your new activity level, allowing you to progress to additional activities. Even more importantly, it will help you begin to think of yourself as an active person.

If you are already active, even a few added steps here and there and a little extra effort during everyday tasks can add up to big benefits. In fact, many people who have conquered their weight challenges have made increased activity a way of life. Look at some simple ways to boost your lifestyle activities and underline the ideas you will try.

At home: Housework such as vacuuming, scrubbing floors, making beds, and washing windows keep your house and your body in shape. Balance on one foot while you are cooking, washing dishes, or brushing your teeth. Instead of piling things at the bottom of the stairs, make a trip upstairs every chance you get. Stretch while you are reading your mail. Do some floor exercises while you watch television or stand up and stretch during the commercials. Even standing while you watch T.V. will burn more calories and build more muscle than just sitting. Tape your favorite daytime show to watch in the evening while you use a treadmill or stationary bike. Better yet, turn off the T.V., turn on some music, and dance. Yard work like mowing your lawn, weeding, and gardening are great, too. Other ideas include washing your car, walking to the mailbox, getting up to change the channels, and walking to the next room to talk instead of yelling.

At work: Get off the bus or subway a stop or two early or park in a distant parking space and walk the rest of the way. Consider walking or riding your bike to work. Use the stairs instead of the elevator; start with one flight once a day and gradually increase until you hardly use the elevator at all. Walk down the hall to your co-worker's office instead of using the intercom, phone, or email. Contract and relax your muscles while you are sitting at your desk. Fidget. Fidgeting, like tapping your foot or bouncing your leg, uses a little energy—just don't drive your co-workers crazy. Stand and stretch or walk around when you need a break. Walk to your meetings and to lunch. Take a walk during your lunch hour or use a nearby gym. Even better, ask a co-worker to join you. See if your employer offers any fitness benefits like an on-site exercise facility or discounts to local clubs. If these aren't presently available, ask for them—everyone benefits from healthier employees.

While out: Do your errands on foot whenever possible. (They don't call it running errands for nothing!) Park your car in a central location and walk to all of your destinations. Walk through the mall briskly. In fact, many malls open early so you can walk in a temperature-controlled environment; take a few laps and window-shop before the stores open. Take the stairs instead of the escalator or elevator. Stretch and tighten your muscles while waiting in lines or sitting at stoplights.

At leisure: Have fun! Play actively with your children or grandchildren. They love to play tag, ride bikes, or practice sports—don't be surprised if you strengthen your relationships too. Walk your dog, play fetch, or chase him around the backyard. Join an adult sports league like softball or bowling. Sign up for a walking, hiking, or jogging club. Walk the golf course and carry your own golf clubs instead of renting a cart. Take up tennis or learn another sport. Take a swim to cool off and relax in the summer or find an indoor pool in the winter.

Reconnect at the end of the day with your partner or a friend on an evening walk. Plan a hike or a walking tour when you have out-of-town visitors. Instead of always going out for a meal, choose dancing, bowling, or other active pursuits with friends.

While traveling: Walk around the airport or conference center instead of sitting around waiting. See the local sights by foot or walk to attractions. Stretch or do exercises in your hotel room and take advantage of the hotel's gym or the resort's exercise classes. Use the stairs and walk to meetings and restaurants. Plan a vacation that includes lots of opportunities to rejuvenate your body as well as your mind.

At rest: Stretch when you wake up and after sitting for a long time. Learn basic yoga or tai chi and practice daily. Try deep breathing exercises, relaxation techniques, and meditation. Give yourself time to relax at the end of the day. Get enough sleep so you will have plenty of energy for your more active lifestyle.

Health Notes: Exercise Clearance

Be safe and consider seeing your doctor to get medical clearance before starting an exercise program. Your doctor will help you determine if you have any underlying medical problems that need to be addressed to be sure that exercise is safe for you. Some of the factors you will want to explore with your physician include your family history and your personal cardiac risk factors such as age, current level of fitness, smoking history, blood pressure, cholesterol levels, diabetes, and other markers for heart disease. You will also want to discuss any musculoskeletal problems and other medical issues that may affect your exercise program. It is very important to seek immediate medical attention if you have symptoms of chest pain, shortness of breath, dizziness, lightheadedness, loss of consciousness, or if you develop those symptoms while exercising. You can use the "Physical Activity Readiness Questionnaire: PAR-Q and You" available at http://www.csep.ca/forms.asp to help you determine whether you should see your doctor before you start an exercise program.

Starting a Fitness Program

As you become more active in your daily life, your body will adapt to the increased demand by becoming more physically fit. When you add activities specifically designed to improve your level of fitness, you will really be amazed at what your body is capable of doing to meet the challenge.

Be smart by starting at an exercise level that is right for you. To do this and still achieve optimal benefit from your fitness program, apply the FITT Principle. FITT stands for Frequency, Intensity, Time, and Type.

- **Frequency:** How often you do the activity.
- **Intensity:** How much effort you use during the activity.
- **Time:** How long you do the activity.
- **Type:** What kind of activity you choose.

You can change any one of these variables to meet your personal fitness health needs and preferences. There are literally thousands of types of physical activity to choose from, but there are three main areas of fitness to build on: cardiorespiratory fitness, muscular strength, and flexibility. The next three chapters will guide you in these areas.

- **Cardiorespiratory activities** raise your heart rate for a sustained period of time and strengthen your heart, lungs, and circulatory system. Examples of this type of activity include walking, jogging, swimming, cycling, and dancing.

- **Strength training** involves resistance activities such as weight training and push-ups which build your muscular strength and endurance, increase your muscle mass and increase your metabolism.

- **Flexibility activities,** including stretching and yoga, improve function and help prevent injury.

For an example of how this works, look at what Leslie discovered.

I never thought I would be a person who actually enjoys exercise. It always seemed so hard and uncomfortable. I swear I would rather have sat at my kitchen table and paid bills then go out for a walk. So, I started out just by looking for ways to do a little more at work and at home. For example, instead of using the intercom system at my office, I just get up and find the person I need. Also, I don't dread vacuuming anymore—I just look at it as a chance to burn a little extra fuel. Once I saw how easy it was to be more active, I decided to start a fitness program. I started by walking 15 minutes about three times a week. By the second week I was doing 20 minutes. By the third week I increased my walks to four or five times a week. I also added some stretching exercises and some push-ups and sit-ups. Believe it or not, I walk almost every day now. I even have a hill near my home that I added to my walks—and I am thinking about pulling the bike I bought a few years ago out of the garage and giving it another try.

If you are already exercising regularly, you have probably discovered its countless benefits. Congratulate yourself. Review your current program to make sure you are obtaining the optimal benefit for your effort. If you don't have a fitness program, here are some key points to keep in mind when getting started:

Start Now: Too often, people wait for the perfect time to begin an exercise program. It is unlikely that the perfect time will ever come—and it won't last forever anyway—so make fitness fit into your life just the way it is today.

Start Small: Assess your current level of fitness then build up gradually from there. Starting with ten to 15 minutes of exercise a day and increasing the time and intensity slowly is the safest and most successful way of incorporating this wonderful habit.

Be Consistent: Consistency is one of the keys to improving your fitness. It is helpful to write down your plan on your calendar or on your "to do" list. Fitness is a process that deserves your commitment to do it consistently.

Set Goals: Small, realistic, achievable goals will encourage you along the way. Set specific goals like a specific number of sessions per week, a certain number of minutes per session, a particular number of steps or repetitions, or even set a lifestyle goal like being able to climb a flight of stairs without feeling breathless.

Stay Motivated: Look for ways to keep yourself motivated since this will be a crucial part of your long-term success. It takes time to see the physical changes that result from increasing your activity, so find ways to reward yourself for your small steps along the way. For example, you could make a graph as you achieve the exercise goals you have set. You could pay yourself a quarter or a dollar every time you complete a session and then spend it on exercise clothing, music, or even a massage or manicure. Regularly review why you want to become more fit.

Have Fun!: Keep your exercise enjoyable and interesting. Choose activities that appeal to you—if you dread it, you won't do it. Change your routine frequently by trying new types of exercise, new locations, and new techniques. Consider finding an exercise buddy, someone who will make exercise more fun and hold you accountable.

By increasing your lifestyle activity and starting a fitness program, you can build your fitness steadily. Anybody can become more active than they are—it just takes desire and creativity.

Nutrition: Essentials of Fluids

Since we aren't going to give you a list of rules to follow about what to eat, you will need to make choices for yourself. That means you need information about your choices and how they affect your body. That is the purpose of the nutrition sections in this book.

The food you eat contains six important classes of nutrients: water, carbohydrates, fats, proteins, vitamins, and minerals. These nutrients serve different functions: some provide energy, some are used in the chemical processes of metabolism, and others are necessary for the growth and replacement of cells. We'll address fluid first.

We start with fluids for a number of good reasons. First, water is essential for optimal health. It may be your body's single most important nutrient since you couldn't survive for more than about a week without it. Second, we focus first on fluids because you'll need to practice identifying the sensations of hunger before focusing on specific foods. Third, people commonly mistake thirst for hunger and therefore eat instead of drink. Last, there are many similarities between hunger and thirst so the concepts will reinforce one another.

The Importance of Water

Approximately 60 percent to 70 percent of your body is comprised of water. That is about ten to 15 gallons! Unfortunately, it is often overlooked and underconsumed. Water is found in every cell, tissue, and organ—nearly every life-sustaining body process requires water to function. Some of these critical activities include:

- Maintaining blood pressure and blood flow
- Digesting food
- Transporting nutrients throughout the body
- Eliminating waste products from the body
- Protecting and lubricating the organs and tissues
- Regulating and maintaining body temperature

In order to ensure that these important functions are carried out, the body attempts to keep this delicate system in balance at all times. Since many people consume far too little water, their bodies must work very hard to maintain this system. Like hunger, you may have learned to ignore the signal of thirst until it becomes very strong, by which time you are already significantly dehydrated.

What Happens When You Consume Too Little of This Critical Nutrient?

If you usually don't drink enough water, your body secretes a hormone called aldosterone in order to conserve water. Aldosterone stimulates your body to hold on to every molecule of water (and sodium) it can. This leads to fluid retention in the tissues and a suppression of thirst, which is why you don't feel thirsty until you are already dehydrated.

When you drink a sufficient amount of water most of the time, your body's production of aldosterone decreases and the excess fluid and sodium are excreted. When this break-through point is reached, you may notice a sudden loss of several pounds, a decrease in the symptoms of fluid retention such as puffiness and swelling, and a return of normal thirst.

Signs of Dehydration

Many people are chronically, mildly dehydrated but have mild or no symptoms. If you continually struggle with fatigue and lack of stamina, you may be living in a state of slight dehydration. Imagine being able to boost your energy level just by consuming a sufficient amount of fluid.

On the other hand, significant dehydration can be very serious—even deadly! Serious dehydration may occur with prolonged fluid restriction or if you don't drink enough fluid during hot or humid weather, exercise, or illness such as vomiting, diarrhea, or fever. Symptoms include irritability, moodiness, fatigue, headaches, dizziness, muscle weakness, cramping, nausea, diarrhea, and confusion. These symptoms require immediate medical attention.

Recommended Fluid Intake

It is usually recommended that you drink eight to 12 eight-ounce glasses of water daily. Since there is a lot of variation among individuals, a practical method to determine how well you are hydrated is to pay attention to the color of your urine.

When you are drinking enough fluid, you will pass plenty of very light yellow or nearly clear urine. When you don't drink enough water, your body must hold on to as much fluid as possible, making your urine more concentrated. In this situation you will pass smaller amounts of urine that look darker in color. (Please note that some vitamins and some medications can also affect the color of your urine.)

Other Factors Affecting Your Fluid Needs

Temperature: Since water helps regulate your body temperature by perspiration through both obvious sweating and imperceptible evaporation, higher body temperatures cause an increased loss of water. This is especially important for people who live in hot climates.

Activity: Any increase in activity will result in more perspiration and loss of water. You must increase your water intake before, during, and after physical activity to avoid dehydration. Be especially mindful of the symptoms of dehydration in yourself and those around you during exercise.

Age: Children and the elderly are more prone to dehydration and the effects of fluid shifts.

Body Weight: The more you weigh, the more fluid you need.

Medical Conditions: Vomiting, diarrhea, high fever, hyperventilation, certain medical conditions, and various medications can lead to the loss or retention of fluids. Medications such as diuretics, commonly known as water pills, should only be used under medical supervision.

Hormones: Women may experience marked fluid shifts as a result of their menstrual cycles, pregnancy, or use of hormonal medications.

Salt Intake: Excessive salt intake leads to more fluid retention. In addition to using less salt during cooking and at the table, watch out for the hidden salt found in processed and convenience foods, and in some beverages including vegetable juices and sodas. Read the labels of food products carefully to determine the salt content (listed as sodium).

Dietary Intake: That initial impressive weight loss on some diets is actually due to fluid loss. Since food is composed of an average of 70 percent water, a sudden decrease in the amount of food intake can result in a temporary loss of water weight. However, your goal should be a loss of fat, not fluid.

Caffeine Intake: Caffeine is a weak diuretic, meaning that your body will lose some fluid when you consume caffeine-containing fluids. Coffee, tea, and sodas with caffeine are considered safe in moderation, which is two to three servings per day.

Essential Information and Practical Strategies

Remember, fluid is essential for weight loss and optimal health. Your fluid intake (especially water) is extremely important for metabolizing fat, giving you a feeling of satisfaction, preventing constipation, decreasing water retention, and improving your energy levels.

First, assess your current fluid intake. Jot down the amount and type of fluid you are taking in. Check the color of your urine—it should be pale. Next, if needed, create a plan for improving the quantity and quality of your fluid intake.

Thirst can be mistaken for hunger. Sometimes an urge to eat is caused by a physical need for water, not food. If your fluid intake has been below par, try a glass of water before reaching for food—especially when you aren't sure that you are hungry.

Increase your water intake. Every day or two, add an additional cup (8 ounces) of water to what you are already drinking. If drinking water is difficult for you, try very cold, bottled or filtered water. For more flavor and interest, try sparkling water or flavored bottled water. Or, add slices of lemon, lime, orange, kiwi, or cucumber, or a few ounces of cranberry juice to enhance the flavor of your water.

Spread your fluids throughout the day. The initial inconvenience of increased trips to the bathroom will improve over time. Keep in mind that the increased urination probably means that your body is letting go of excess fluids more easily. You may find that it is better to stop drinking fluids well before bedtime if you have to get up at night to urinate.

Keep your water within easy reach. If water is handy, you are more likely to drink it. Some easy ideas: keep a 16 or 24 ounce water bottle at your desk, in your car, or with you at home, and set a goal to drink it and refill it every two to three hours; drink an 8-ounce glass of water every hour, or before and between each meal; keep a half-gallon jug of water in the refrigerator and commit yourself to finishing it off before the end of the day; make a trip to the water cooler every time you take a break from work; never pass a water fountain without taking a drink; add ice to your beverages so that as it melts, it will give you even more fluid.

Watch your sodium (salt) intake. If your salt intake is excessive, you will retain more water in your tissues. For some people, this can even lead to elevated blood pressure and other medical problems.

Decrease your caffeine intake. Watch your serving sizes of caffeinated drinks since they are often served in large mugs or cups. If you are drinking more than two or three servings of caffeinated beverages such as coffee or soda per day, begin to decrease gradually to avoid caffeine withdrawal headaches. Every few days, try cutting out one serving or replacing it with a caffeine-free version ...

Drink more water before, during, and after you exercise. Since exercise is so important in helping you manage your weight, don't forget to increase your water intake to replace fluid losses as you increase your activity level.

Some fluids have nutritional value. Low fat or skim milk, protein drinks, meal replacement beverages, real fruit juice, and fruit smoothies pack valuable nutrients along with their fluid. However, be aware of their caloric content as well.

Some fluids are actually food. Popular specialty coffee drinks and commercial smoothies often have a lot of fat and sugar in them—and a chocolate shake is really just liquefied ice cream. The problem is that, for some people, drinking food doesn't completely satisfy their hunger because they didn't get to chew anything.

Be aware that some fluids contribute calories and can make it harder to lose weight. Sugar-laden soft drinks and fruit-flavored drinks have 150 calories or more per serving. Eliminating just one a day could result in up to 18 pounds of weight loss in a year. You can accomplish this by gradually replacing them with water. Keep in mind that soft drinks may also have a lot of sodium, which can cause fluid retention and carbonation, which can lead to gas and bloating.

Some foods are high in fluids too. Although water is the best source for keeping hydrated, many foods have a high water content, especially fruits, vegetables, and soups.

Consider whether you prefer to drink or eat your calories. You may find that you are more satisfied by having an orange and a glass of water than by drinking a glass of orange juice.

Sports drinks are for strenuous sports. Sports drinks are best for use during intense exercise lasting more than one hour, since they provide fluid with electrolytes and sugar. They are not recommended for average activity or when you are watching your sodium and calorie intake.

Watch the extras! The sugar, sweetener, creamer, flavorings, and other extras that you add to your beverages can really add up without really satisfying your hunger.

What about alcohol? Because of the way your body processes alcohol, it will not help hydrate your body. In fact, it can actually cause dehydration. It also contains a significant number of calories—7 calories per gram, compared to protein and carbohydrates, which have 4, and fat which has 9. Further, its effects may interfere with your ability to make healthy decisions about your food choices.

Don't be discouraged by fluctuations in your weight that may be due to fluid retention. Instead, focus on further increasing your water intake to help your body excrete the extra salt and fluid. If this is an ongoing problem for you, seek medical advice.

Don't be surprised if you develop a strong preference for water. Once you are in the habit of drinking it, you will find that nothing satisfies thirst as well as water. Taking these important steps to increase your fluid intake is critical for building optimal health and wellness. Drink up.

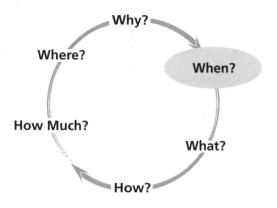

CHAPTER 4

Decision Point: How Hungry Am I?

As you have become accustomed to using hunger to guide your eating, you probably noticed that it is not only important to notice *whether* you are hungry, but *how* hungry you are. The Hunger and Fullness Scale is a useful tool to help assess your hunger levels before, during, and after eating. It will help you identify hunger cues, observe how different types and amounts of food affect you, and help you recognize when the urge to eat has been triggered by something other than hunger. This scale is not intended to set strict guidelines about when you should eat but rather, to help you develop awareness of your body's natural signals of hunger and fullness.

The Hunger and Fullness Scale ranges from 1 to 10. In the middle of the scale is 5, which is satisfied and comfortable. At a 5, you cannot feel your stomach at all. It is neither empty nor full; it is not growling or feeling stretched. This may be how your stomach feels after you have eaten breakfast. Most people don't want to feel sluggish in the morning, so they tend to eat light, resulting in a comfortable level of satiety.

The Hunger and Fullness Scale

Ravenous	Starving	Hungry	Pangs	Satisfied	Full	Very Full	Discomfort	Stuffed	Sick
1	2	3	4	5	6	7	8	9	10

The numbers less than 5 represent how hungry you are (remember: smaller numbers, smaller stomach) while the numbers above 5 represent how full you are (remember: larger numbers, larger stomach). For example, a 1 represents ravenous—you are so hungry that you could eat this book. A 10 indicates that you are so full that you are in pain and feel sick. The other numbers represent various degrees of hunger or fullness between ravenous and sick.

At first, you may have difficulty labeling various levels of hunger with these numbers, but with frequent practice it will become second nature. Here are some descriptions that will help you learn what the numbers represent:

1 **Ravenous:** Too hungry to care what you eat, you are at high risk for overeating.

2 **Starving:** You feel that you must eat NOW!

3 **Hungry:** Eating would be pleasurable, but you could wait longer.

4 **Hunger pangs:** You are slightly hungry; your first thoughts of food emerge.

5 **Satisfied:** You are content, comfortable—not hungry, not full—you cannot feel your stomach at all.

6 **Full:** You can feel the food in your stomach.

7 **Very full:** Your stomach feels stretched and you feel sleepy and sluggish.

8 **Uncomfortable:** Your stomach is too full and you wish you hadn't eaten so much.

9 **Stuffed:** Your clothes feel very tight and you are very uncomfortable.

10 **Sick:** You feel sick and/or you are in pain.

It helps to develop a good mental picture of what is happening to your stomach at these different levels of hunger and fullness. Think of a large balloon.

Hunger and Fullness

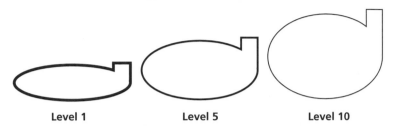

| Level 1 | Level 5 | Level 10 |

When the balloon is completely empty, it is almost flat. This would be a 1. When you blow that first puff of air into the balloon, it takes its shape as it fills out gently to hold the air. This would be a 5. So, think of the size of your stomach as the amount of food that it takes to go from a 1 to a 5.

As you take a deep breath and force more air into a balloon, its elastic walls begin to stretch and expand. This would be levels 6 through 10. Your stomach is able to stretch to a 10 in order to hold excess food; therefore the numbers over 5 indicate how stretched or uncomfortable your stomach feels. If you blow too much air in, the balloon stretches even larger and eventually pops. Fortunately, stomachs rarely rupture, but most of us have eaten so much at one time or another that we have said, "If I eat one more bite, I will explode!" When you feel this way, you are at a 10.

Of course, hunger and fullness are also signaled by changes in blood sugar levels, energy levels, moods, and substances in the bloodstream resulting from the digestive process as we discussed in Chapter 2. Make an effort to pay attention to these and other clues when determining how hungry or full you are.

To summarize, whenever you have an urge to eat, ask yourself, "Am I hungry?" Focus on your physical sensations, thoughts, and feelings. Use the Hunger and Fullness Scale to choose a number that seems to represent how hungry, satisfied, or full you are. If you are a 4 or below, you are hungry; if you are 5 or higher, you are not. It is that simple.

Practice identifying and quantifying your hunger. As this skill becomes more automatic, you will move closer to becoming the expert on meeting your body's needs.

When Should I Eat?

Once you can identify your signals of hunger, satisfaction, and fullness, you can begin to fine-tune your eating patterns.

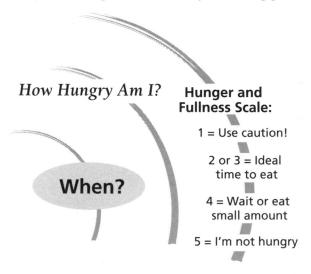

How Hungry Am I? **Hunger and Fullness Scale:**

1 = Use caution!

2 or 3 = Ideal time to eat

When?

4 = Wait or eat small amount

5 = I'm not hungry

1: If you put off eating or don't notice that you are hungry until you are at a 1, then you will be more likely to eat anything you can get your hands on. You are also more likely to eat too quickly to notice when you are satisfied, so you are more likely to overeat.

2 or 3: The ideal time to begin eating is when you reach a 3 or 2. At this point you are significantly hungry and food will be pleasurable and satisfying.

4: When your hunger level is a 4, you are slightly hungry and having your first thoughts of food. This means that you will need to eat in awhile so you can begin to plan for it by making sure that time and food will be available when you are ready. If you eat right away when you reach a 4, it will take only a small amount of food to satisfy you. Therefore, you may find that it is easy to overeat if you eat before you are significantly hungry.

5 or Higher: If you are a 5 or above and you have an urge to eat or keep eating, you know that something other than hunger triggered it. Recognizing this will give you an opportunity to learn more about yourself and how you respond to your environment and your emotions.

The Rhythms of Hunger

Up to this point, we have examined the basics of hunger. However, there are many other nuances that can help you understand your personal hunger rhythms.

It may take 20 to 30 minutes after eating for you to recognize your level of fullness. People commonly tell us that they thought they were satisfied when they finished eating, but felt full a short time later. If you tend to overshoot and eat too much, slow down, chew your food thoroughly, and put your fork down between bites. This may slow your food intake down enough to allow the physical sensations to catch up with your awareness of satisfaction. Stop periodically in the middle of eating to ask yourself where you are on the Hunger and Fullness Scale. It is also helpful to try to stop eating before you actually feel satisfied. You can always eat again later if you need to.

Hunger cannot be satisfied before it occurs. You cannot eat now to satisfy hunger that is yet to come. Eating even though you are not hungry, to prevent feeling hungry later at an inconvenient time, is called preventive eating. The food you eat when you are not hungry will usually be stored as excess fat to be used later. If you already have fat stores, there is no reason to build them up even further with preventive eating.

Think of it like this. If you are comfortable in a room but you put on a heavy coat now because you may get cold in an hour, you will probably get hot and become uncomfortable in the meantime. Instead, if you wait until you feel cold, then the coat will do what it is supposed to do—make you warm and keep you comfortable. Hunger works the same way. If you eat now because you may get hungry in an hour, you will feel full and uncomfortable. If you wait to eat until you are hungry, you will feel comfortable and satisfied.

Preventative eating may be a result of a fear of hunger. You may have become so out of touch with your natural feelings of hunger that you view them as unpleasant and something to be avoided. To combat this fear, assure yourself that you will usually be able to eat when you are hungry.

Try to be prepared for hunger at all times by carrying food (preferably a healthy, satisfying choice) with you wherever you go. Promise yourself that you can eat when you are physically hungry so there is no need to overeat to try to prevent hunger.

It is also helpful to remember that occasionally feeling hungry won't hurt you; in fact, it will help you become better aware of your hunger cues and it will cause your body to use some of its fat stores. In other words, it is better to be hungry for a little while than to eat when you are not truly hungry and force your body to make more fat.

Hunger can be postponed if food is not available or it is not convenient to eat. If you can't eat when you first get hungry, the hunger may disappear and return in an hour or two. This is very useful since it is not always possible or convenient to eat when you first become hungry as we discussed above. Keep in mind though, if you take advantage of this and ignore hunger too often, it may backfire and cause your metabolism to slow down in order to conserve energy.

Hunger does not follow a clock. If you tell yourself, "I should be hungry; it's dinnertime" or "I shouldn't be hungry yet," then you are not listening to your body. Hunger often occurs even if it is not a conventional mealtime.

However, since it is not always convenient to eat when your hunger tells you to, you may need to retrain yourself to be hungry around a particular time. For instance, if you are usually hungry at four in the afternoon but you want to be hungry for dinner with your family, plan a light afternoon snack so you won't be ravenous by dinnertime. Or maybe you aren't very hungry during your lunch hour. Try eating a little more protein at breakfast so you can skip your mid-morning snack, or just eat a smaller amount at lunch and be prepared to have a mid-afternoon snack.

On the other hand, you might not be hungry when you should be. For example, most diets say you must eat breakfast. It is true that breakfast is a very important meal to spark your internal thermostat and give you energy. However, you may not feel hungry when you first wake up. There is no harm in waiting an hour or two, as long as you are prepared with something to eat once you are hungry and it is convenient to eat.

As you begin to understand how your body responds to different types and amounts of food, you will find that there are lots of ways to train your hunger to fit into your schedule.

Hunger may seem erratic. Hunger comes and goes according to your body's needs. You may feel hungry frequently one day and rarely the next day. For example, many women experience wide fluctuations in their hunger throughout their menstrual cycles due to changing hormone levels. You simply don't need the same type or amount of food at the same time each day.

This is yet another reason that diets so often fail. In the past, you may have been more likely to "cheat" when your hunger didn't match the rules of whatever diet you were following. This time you can become your own expert by learning to understand and trust your body's signals.

Eating small meals satisfies hunger best. Since your stomach is about the size of your fist, it only takes a palm-full of food to fill it without overstretching it. When you don't overfill your stomach, you will feel light and comfortable after eating. This is a very important and useful visual concept. To better picture this, gently make a fist and hold it at the level of your upper abdomen where your stomach lies. Now open you hand and look at your palm. That is about the volume of food it takes for your stomach to go from a 1 or 2 to a 5. Surprising isn't it when you think about how large most of our serving sizes are? No wonder people struggle so much with their weight.

Of course, when you eat a palm-sized amount of food, you are likely to become hungry more often throughout the day. This is why so many people who eat instinctively seem to be eating all of the time. This is also where the common diet rule "eat six small meals a day" originated. However, instead of using an arbitrary schedule suggested by a diet expert, it is more effective to listen to your body and eat an appropriate amount in response to your hunger signals.

Eating frequent small meals reassures your metabolism that food is available to meet its needs. When you eat small amounts frequently, you may experience fewer mood and energy swings. Frequent eating according to your hunger cues also decreases binge eating.

Hunger is affected by what you eat, not just by how much you eat. The types of nutrients the food contains, the number of calories, and the form of the food all affect your hunger levels. Macronutrients (carbohydrates, proteins, and fats) are digested at different rates, so the type of foods you eat may affect how long it takes for you to become hungry again. For example, crackers with peanut butter will last longer than plain crackers. In addition, certain types of nutrients cause the release of certain bio-chemicals that increase satiety. For example, a palm-full of broccoli will feel differently than a palm-full of chocolate candy. When you are really listening to your body, these factors will affect the amount of certain types of food that you eat and how often you feel hungry.

Hunger may be specific for a certain type of food. Often, when you are physically hungry, a specific food will come to mind. As you become familiar with your body's signals, you will begin to recognize what type of food or taste will match your particular hunger at that time. In the next chapter we will look at the factors involved in making your food choice.

Putting It All Together

Let's retrace the steps in your new system so far. Whenever you have an urge to eat, ask yourself, "Am I hungry?" Notice the physical signs of hunger and any associated thoughts and feelings. If you are not hungry, you have three choices: eat anyway, distract yourself, or determine what your true needs are.

If you are hungry, determine how hungry you are by using a number on the Hunger and Fullness Scale then decide if it is an appropriate time to eat. Keep in mind, if you eat when you are a 5 or above, your body does not need the food and you are not eating to satisfy hunger. If you are a 4, it will take only a small amount of food to reach satiation so it may be easier to overeat. A 2 or a 3 is the ideal time to eat since food is likely to be pleasurable and satisfying. If you wait until you are a 1 to eat, proceed with caution; when you are ravenous, you may be more likely to overeat.

You will also use the Hunger and Fullness Scale to determine how much to eat and how to tell when you have overeaten. We will explore this further in the chapter "Am I Satisfied?" In the meantime, practice using the Hunger and Fullness Scale to guide your portion sizes and help you gain optimal satisfaction from eating.

Fitness: Essentials of Cardiorespiratory Fitness

Hopefully you are already convinced of the benefits of exercise for good health, well-being, and weight management. Let's first focus on cardiorespiratory fitness.

Simply put, cardiorespiratory exercise, commonly called cardio, is any activity that strengthens your heart, lungs, and vascular system and improves circulation throughout your body. This type of exercise is often referred to as aerobic, which means with oxygen. That is because it allows you to maintain an elevated heart rate (pulse) for a continuous period of time, without making you feel breathless. On the other hand, anaerobic activities such as weight lifting demand more oxygen than your blood can deliver, so they cannot be kept up for very long.

The Benefits of Cardiorespiratory Fitness

Cardiorespiratory activity will provide you with numerous health benefits:

- Conditions your heart, lungs, and vascular systems.
- Lowers your blood pressure and resting pulse.
- Raises your level of HDL cholesterol—the good kind of cholesterol.
- Lowers your risk for cardiovascular diseases such as heart attack, stroke, and atherosclerosis (hardening of the arteries).
- Increases your stamina.
- Helps you lose excess body fat.
- Tones your major muscles.
- Improves your sense of well-being.
- Improves your sleep.
- Boosts your energy level.

Live longer, look better, and feel great—sounds wonderful, doesn't it? It is! So let's get started.

What You Need to Know

There are many activities that can be considered aerobic including walking, cycling, water aerobics, swimming, low-impact aerobics, hiking, jogging, skating, stair stepping, singles tennis, rowing, cross-country skiing, trampoline, jumping rope, basketball, soccer, and many others. As you can see, this list includes many different types of activities for all fitness levels—so there is something for everybody.

The key is, no matter which activity you choose, the goal is to keep your heart rate up without completely losing your breath. Since everyone has different fitness levels, an activity that is aerobic for one person may be anaerobic for the next person. For example, jogging might be a perfect activity for a person who exercises regularly, while a person who is just getting started may feel totally winded within a short period of time and have to quit. This person would instead benefit far more from walking. The point is, start at your own level of fitness in order to reap the full benefit of whatever activity you choose.

Once you have been cleared by your doctor to begin to exercise, plan a cardiorespiratory exercise program that meets your needs. The most important thing is to choose one or more activities that you are likely to enjoy. Many people choose to start their cardiorespiratory exercise by walking, so we'll use that as our example. However, if walking is not a good activity for you, choose something else and apply the same principles: start slowly, be consistent, and keep it interesting.

Getting Started

Walking is an ideal activity for almost any fitness level, at just about any weight. You can walk just about anywhere, anytime, with minimal equipment needed—just a comfortable pair of shoes. Consider the following factors:

- **Shoes:** Wear comfortable shoes with flexible thick soles, preferably shoes that have been designed for walking. You don't have to spend a lot of money, but it is helpful to speak to an experienced salesperson if you tend to have foot problems. And remember, the support inside your walking shoes will be worn out long before they look worn out on the outside.

- **Clothing:** Comfortable, light cotton clothing will absorb sweat and allow evaporation in the summer. Layer clothing in the winter since you will quickly warm up with activity. Don't be too concerned with how you *look*—the goal is to *feel* good.

- **Sun Protection:** Don't forget to wear a hat, sunscreen, and sunglasses with UVA and UVB protection during the peak hours of the day, even during the winter.

- **Location:** If possible, your neighborhood is best for starters since that will be the most convenient. Having a treadmill at home makes it convenient to walk anytime. For variety and interest, walk to, or in, other nearby neighborhoods, parks, malls, and trails. Look for smooth, even surfaces if you are not very surefooted. Surfaces softer than concrete may help absorb shock and will be more comfortable. Try a running track or walk on the asphalt rather than the sidewalk—of course being very mindful of traffic.

- **Safety:** Walk in the daytime or in well-lit areas. Wear reflective clothing or shoes if you walk at night. Stay aware of your surroundings. Walking with a partner provides additional security. Let others know your route and expected time of return and take a mobile phone with you, if possible. Consider carrying pepper spray and a whistle or another type of alarm to use in case you are in danger.

- **Partners:** If you like the idea of sharing your walk with someone else, or if you think it will help keep you motivated, ask someone to join you. Choose one or more partners who can walk on the same schedule and who are at about the same level of fitness or higher. This is a great chance to spend quality time with someone—and it definitely makes the time go faster. Sometimes pets or children on bikes or in strollers make good partners too—just don't let them slow you down too much.

- **Proper Walking Technique:** Walk with your head and chin up and your shoulders held slightly back. Your heel should touch the ground first then roll your weight forward. Make sure your toes point straight ahead. Swing your arms as you walk, either down at your side, or with your elbows flexed to 90 degrees with your fist swinging up to the level of your breastbone.

Get FITT

Walking is a fun and very effective way to get fit. By adjusting the *frequency* (how often), *intensity* (how much effort you use), *time* (how long you walk), and type (choice of walking as an activity), you can create a program that is just right for you.

Frequency: Plan to walk most days of the week. While three days per week improves cardiorespiratory health, you will want to walk more often if your goal is to lose weight. Remember, you can also break your walk into several shorter sessions if you are too busy or not used to exercising—you will still gain the same benefits.

At the beginning of the week, schedule your walks and write them down on your calendar. Once you have committed yourself to those times, give them the priority they deserve. If you have to cancel, reschedule just as you would any other important appointment. Most people find it easier to be consistent when they exercise first thing in the morning, before other distractions get in the way. Of course, the bonus is increased energy and less stress throughout the rest of the day.

Intensity: Your fitness level will determine how fast you walk. The goal is to use enough effort to challenge your body so it will become more fit. Each session should be composed of four parts:

- **Warm Up:** Walk slowly for five minutes and allow your muscles to warm up by increasing circulation. Please note that warming up is not the same thing as stretching. Stretching should only be done after the muscles are warm, for example, at the end of your walk.

- **Brisk Walk:** Gradually increase your speed as you begin to feel energetic. You should be able to carry on a conversation—but if you can sing, go a little faster. As you become more fit, add a few extra minutes to your walk and walk a little faster.

- **Cool down:** Walk slowly for 5 minutes to allow your muscles to cool down and your circulation to return to normal.

- **Stretching:** Stretching after your warm up and again at the end of your walk will help prevent injuries. Chapter 5 provides the details to get you started with stretching.

Time: The sample schedule below is one way to build your cardiovascular fitness. If you haven't been exercising regularly, start at the top and gradually work your way up to 20 to 60 minutes a day. If you are already exercising, simply choose the starting point that matches your current fitness level and go from there. This is just a sample—so make adjustments to meet your needs. Again, try to walk most days of the week. You can also use this sample chart to build activities other than walking.

Sample Walking Schedule:

WEEK	WARM-UP	BRISK WALK	COOL DOWN	TOTAL TIME	STRETCHING
1	5 min	5 min	5 min	15 min	After walk
2	5 min	7 min	5 min	17 min	After walk
3	5 min	10 min	5 min	20 min	After walk
4	5 min	12 min	5 min	22 min	After walk
5	5 min	15 min	5 min	25 min	After walk
6	5 min	18 min	5 min	28 min	After walk
7	5 min	21 min	5 min	31 min	After walk
8	5 min	24 min	5 min	34 min	After walk
9	5 min	27 min	5 min	37 min	After walk
10	5 min	30 min	5 min	40 min	After walk
11	5 min	33 min	5 min	43 min	After walk
12	5 min	35 min	5 min	45 min	After walk

Type: In addition to walking, try other aerobic activities like swimming, cycling, hiking, jogging, rowing, cross-country skiing, singles tennis, exercise classes, exercise tapes, dancing, and others. Check with your local community education departments, community colleges, and fitness facilities for additional offerings.

Keep It Interesting

- Don't let boredom derail your plan. Make small changes to your regular routine often. For example, once in awhile try a longer session, a different time of day, a new route, or even your same route backwards.

- Try meditative walking to clear your mind while you are exercising your body. For example, inhale slowly for four steps, hold for one step, exhale slowly for four steps, and then hold for one step. Repeat.

- As you become more fit, continually challenge yourself. You can increase how long and how frequently you walk *and* increase the intensity of your walk. By going faster, moving your arms, pushing a stroller, or walking uphill, your fitness level will continue to improve.

- A pedometer is a fun way to measure your activity level throughout the day. It is a small device that is worn on your waist to measure the number of steps you take, making it easy to set small goals for yourself. It is motivating to see those steps add up—and see your energy level rise as your fitness improves. Pedometers are available just about anywhere that you can purchase fitness and sports equipment.

- Try new cardiorespiratory activities. This keeps you from getting bored and utilizes different muscle groups to improve your overall fitness. If you usually walk, try gentle hiking or jogging for short periods of time during your walk.

Building your cardiovascular fitness has many benefits for your health, your weight, and your energy. Choose an activity you think you will enjoy, create a plan, and keep it interesting. By taking it one step at a time, you will find yourself on your way to optimal health.

Nutrition: Essentials of Carbohydrates

Carbohydrates are an important family of nutrients that provide your body with energy. In addition to energy, many carbohydrate-containing foods also provide fiber, important vitamins, minerals, and phyto-chemicals that have been shown to improve health.

Carbohydrates are found in bread and other grain products, fruits, vegetables, and dairy products. Since carbohydrates are found in many different foods, they are great for adding variety and flavor to your diet.

Most dietary guidelines, including the 2000 Dietary Guidelines for Healthy Americans, which has also been endorsed by the American Dietetic Association and American Heart Association, recommend that 50 percent to 60 percent of your total daily calorie intake come from carbohydrates. Recent recommendations from the Institute of Medicine encourage a broader, more flexible range of 45 percent to 65 percent. According to all of these authorities the majority of your food intake should be carbohydrates.

The Role of Carbohydrates in Your Health

At some point, you may have heard someone say, "Carbohydrates just turn to sugar in your body." Since many people think of sugar as "bad," they think of carbohydrates as "bad." But actually, sugar is just another word for glucose, which is an important form of energy for your body. So, the truth is, the majority of carbohydrates do turn into sugar during digestion. But that is what they are supposed to do. To understand why that is not "bad," a brief biochemistry lesson is in order.

Carbohydrates found in our foods are manufactured by plants. Carbohydrates are primarily made up of molecules called glucose. When carbohydrates are eaten and digested, they are broken down to this simple form—glucose. Glucose then floats in your bloodstream (hence the term blood sugar), where it is ready to be taken up by your cells to be used for energy or stored. Under normal circumstances, your body closely regulates your blood glucose (or blood sugar) levels.

When your blood glucose rises after eating, your pancreas releases insulin. Insulin has two main jobs. It stimulates your brain, muscle, fat, and other cells to take up glucose to be used for fuel. It also stimulates the liver to make glycogen, the storage form of glucose. These functions keep your blood sugar stable and make sure that your body has glucose available for fuel when needed. About one to three hours after eating, blood sugar and insulin levels both return to baseline.

When you haven't eaten in awhile your blood sugar levels begin to fall. You may experience moodiness, irritability, fatigue, nausea, headaches, and an inability to concentrate. This is partly due to the fact that red blood cells and most brain cells depend on glucose to function. To keep your blood sugar levels from falling too low, your pancreas releases a hormone called glucagon. Glucagon breaks glycogen back down into glucose so that fuel is available.

What Happens When You Don't Eat Enough Carbohydrates

If you don't eat enough carbohydrates to supply your cells with glucose and maintain a store of glycogen, your body is forced to make glucose from other nutrients. However, your body cannot make glucose from fat so it will use protein from the food you eat and protein from your muscles. As a result, some of the protein in your diet will be used to make glucose, instead of making tissues and performing other vital functions. In addition, since your body will break down protein from your muscles, heart, liver, kidneys, and other vital organs to be turned into necessary glucose, you will lose valuable lean body mass, which can have long-term damaging effects on your metabolism. Further, when you regain weight, you regain fat, not the lost muscle tissue.

Carbohydrates are also important for the breakdown of fat. When there aren't enough carbohydrates in your diet, partial breakdown products of fat, called ketones, are formed. The brain uses these ketones for energy. However this condition, known as ketosis, disturbs the body's normal acid-base balance and can lead to other health problems. It may also decrease the appetite and cause nausea, dizziness, diarrhea, fatigue, bad breath, and headaches.

Admittedly, this explanation is actually a bit of an oversimplification. The main point is that carbohydrates are an important and significant source of fuel for your body. Understanding how your body functions and uses this fuel will help you make the best possible decisions for yourself.

Health Notes: Metabolic Syndrome

Many overweight individuals develop insulin resistance, a situation in which their tissues ignore insulin signals. Insulin resistance allows the blood glucose levels to remain too high. The body tries to compensate for these high glucose levels by producing even more insulin, resulting in hyperinsulinemia. These high insulin levels promote fat storage and inhibit fat burning.

Hyperinsulinemia contributes to the development of Metabolic Syndrome, also called Insulin Resistance Syndrome or Syndrome X. This syndrome is characterized by abdominal obesity (waist measurement more than 40 inches in men or 35 inches in women), high blood pressure, high triglycerides, low HDL ("good" cholesterol), and high fasting blood sugars. Metabolic Syndrome is important because it increases the risk of developing diabetes and heart disease.

Diabetes is a disease in which the blood glucose levels are too high, either because there isn't enough insulin (called Type I) or because the body isn't using insulin properly as explained above (called Type II). Diabetes causes damage to important tissues, leading to heart disease, kidney failure, blindness, and amputations. Many overweight people develop diabetes and 79 percent of diabetics are overweight or obese.

There is ongoing research into the relationship between diet and Metabolic Syndrome. Until there are definite answers, here are a few irrefutable facts when it comes to managing insulin and blood sugar levels:

- When you consume more calories than your body needs, you will increase your fat stores, which increases your risk of metabolic syndrome. It doesn't matter if the extra energy comes from carbohydrates, protein, or fat.

- Exercise decreases insulin resistance. If your glycogen stores are full from eating and you don't do any activity to use them up, your body has no need to store the extra glucose that is floating in your bloodstream, so it will be more resistant to the action of insulin. However, when activity depletes the glycogen stored in the muscles and liver, insulin helps these tissues take up glucose from the bloodstream to replenish it.

- Weight loss is the most effective way of improving insulin resistance. This is why a diabetic's blood sugar often dramatically improves as they lose weight. When you decrease your caloric intake and lose weight, your blood sugar and insulin levels will decrease, decreasing your risk of diabetes, high cholesterol, high blood pressure, and heart disease.

From Simple to Complex

Every living cell in your body requires fuel for existence. Carbohydrates play a significant role in meeting those needs by providing necessary energy. Energy from food is measured in kilocalories, which is commonly just called calories. Each gram of carbohydrate provides four calories of energy. For the sake of comparison, protein also provides four calories per gram, while fat provides nine calories per gram.

Essentially, there are two types of carbohydrates: simple and complex. Both are made up of glucose molecules, but they are arranged differently.

Simple Carbohydrates: Also known as simple sugars, simple carbohydrates are small packages of glucose that are broken down easily and rapidly by your body. Simple carbohydrates include fructose found in fruits and honey, lactose found in dairy products, and sucrose found in table sugar, corn syrup, and some vegetables. Consuming a simple carbohydrate when you are hungry, such as a piece of fruit, glass of juice, or candy will give you a quick, but short, burst of energy. This is because simple carbohydrates can be digested and used for energy in a short period of time.

Simple Carbohydrates at a Glance

Carbs	Sources	Examples	Typical Serving Sizes	Grams of Fiber
Fructose	Fruit	Apples, citrus, peaches	1 medium piece of fruit	3
		Banana,	or 1/2 cup chopped	2
		Berries	3-5	
		Melons, tropical fruit	1-2	
		Fruit juice	3/4 cup (6 oz.)	0-1
	Honey	Table honey	1 tablespoon	0
		Honey added to foods	Varies	
Lactose	Dairy	Milk	1 cup (8 oz.)	0
		Soft cheeses (i.e. cottage)	1/2 cup (4 oz.)	
		Hard cheeses (i.e. cheddar)	1 1/2 to 2 oz.	
		Yogurt	1 cup (8 oz.)	
		Ice cream	1/2 cup	
Sucrose	Sugar	Table sugar	1 teaspoon	0
		Corn syrup, table syrup	1 tablespoon	

Complex Carbohydrates: These are larger, more complex forms of carbohydrates. They are made of long chains of simpler carbohydrates linked together—hundreds to thousands of glucose molecules. Complex carbohydrates fall into two main categories: starch and fiber.

Starches are the digestible complex carbohydrates, which means they can be broken down into glucose molecules by your body and used for energy. This breakdown process actually burns calories too. Starches are found in grains, including wheat, rice, barley, and oats. They are also found in products made from grain, such as bread, pasta, tortillas, and cereal. Starches are also found in legumes such as beans, lentils, and nuts, and in vegetables, such as potatoes, corn, and peas. Although the digestion process takes longer than for simple carbohydrates, starch eventually breaks down into glucose (or sugar) that can be used by your body for energy.

Complex Carbohydrates at a Glance

Carbs	Sources	Examples	Typical Serving Sizes	Grams of Fiber
Starch	Unrefined (Whole) Grains and Grain Products	Whole grains (i.e. brown or wild rice, barley)	1/2 cup	2-5
		Unrefined grain products Whole-wheat pasta	1/2 cup	2-5
		Bread, tortilla	1 slice, 1 6-inch tortilla	2-5
		Crackers	6 crackers	2-5
		Cereal	1 oz. (usually 3/4 cup)	3-7
	Refined (Processed) Grains	White rice, pasta	1/2 cup	1/2 -1
		White bread, tortillas	1 slice, 1 6-inch tortilla	1
		Cereals (refined)	1 oz. (often 3/4 cup)	1/2 -1
	Legumes	Beans, lentils	1/2 cup	5-7
		Nuts	1/3 cup	2
		Peanut butter	2 tablespoons	2
	High Starch Vegetables	Peas	1/2 cup	5
		Corn	1/2 cup	2
		Potatoes	1 small (with peel)	2
		Winter Squash	1/2 cup	6
	Low Starch Vegetables	Raw or cooked	1/2 cup chopped	1-3
		Leafy vegetables	1 cup	1
		Juice	3/4 cup (6 oz.)	0-1

Fiber is the term used for indigestible complex carbohydrates. The human body cannot break down the chemical links between the glucose molecules in fiber. This means that fiber does not provide energy in the form of calories. Therefore, fiber helps fill you up without providing any fuel.

Fiber accompanies the starch in plant foods and the simple sugars in fruits. Therefore, it can be found in whole grains, legumes, vegetables, and fruits. Some processed foods are fortified with fiber too. Eating enough fiber will promote smoother digestion, aid in preventing constipation, prevent certain diseases of the colon, help regulate blood sugar levels, and possibly even prevent certain types of cancer. In addition, much research supports the beneficial effects of the fiber found in whole-oat, barley, and rye products in reducing blood cholesterol levels.

Getting the Most from Carbohydrates

Many health authorities, including the 2000 Dietary Guidelines for Healthy Americans, the American Dietetic Association, and the American Diabetic Association, promote at least 6 servings of grains or grain products, 2 to 3 servings of fruits, 3 to 5 servings of vegetables, and 2 to 3 servings of dairy products per day. These recommendations are intended to provide an adequate amount of carbohydrates, fiber, and accompanying vitamins and minerals. The specific recommendation for fiber intake is 25 to 30 grams per day. Numerous studies have shown significant health benefits from consuming a diet high in fruits, vegetables, whole grain, and fiber including reduced risk of cardiovascular disease and cancer.

Remember balance, variety, and moderation. As you now recognize, carbohydrates are found in a diverse group of foods. Carbohydrate-rich foods are an important source of energy and beneficial nutrients. In fact, eating carbohydrates is the only way you can meet your recommended daily fiber intake without taking fiber supplements. Since carbohydrate-containing foods vary in their nutrient and fiber content, choosing a variety of foods will maximize the likelihood that you will meet your body's needs. However, many people eat more carbohydrates than their body actually needs—particularly sugar and refined products. Once again, moderation is the key.

Be aware of your portions sizes. Carbohydrates are important nutrients but it is essential to pay attention to the size and number of servings you eat. For example, a bagel is often three to five servings of bread and a large plate of spaghetti may have three or more servings of pasta. Pay attention to your hunger and satisfaction scale; it is likely that your body knows when the portion size is too large.

Focus on fruits and vegetables. Not only are fruits and vegetables packed with nourishment, they will also help fill you up, satisfy your cravings for sweets, and boost your fiber intake. Here are some ideas to help you meet your nutritional needs:

- On your next visit to the grocery store, pick up fruits or vegetables that you have never tried.
- If you can't eat fresh, frozen is second best for maximum nutrient content.
- Eat skins and peels (thoroughly washed) to increase fiber and other nutrient intake.
- Fruits and vegetables with deeply colored flesh generally have more micronutrients. Some examples: mangoes, blueberries, cantaloupe, tomatoes, and red peppers.
- Darker green leafy and other types of lettuce have more fiber and micronutrients than iceberg lettuce. Try mixing them together at first if you aren't used to the stronger flavors.
- Fresh fruit is always an excellent choice for a snack or dessert.
- Top pancakes with sliced fruit instead of syrup.
- Refresh with a healthy shake—blend skim milk, fruit, and ice.
- Slice an apple or banana in place of jelly on a peanut butter sandwich.
- Top frozen yogurt or sherbet with your favorite fruits.
- Freeze seedless grapes, bananas, strawberries or peach slices for an icy treat.

- Dried fruit is a convenient, sweet, high-fiber snack.
- Remember, whole fruit has more fiber than fruit juice that has been strained.
- If you drink juice, look for 100 percent fruit juice instead of fruit-flavored drinks and check the label for added sugar (or better yet, make your own from fresh fruit, leaving the peels on whenever possible).
- A glass of tomato or vegetable juice is a great pick-me-up.
- Add chopped broccoli, mushrooms, squash, or other veggies to rice, pasta, and stuffing mixes.
- Add extra frozen vegetables to low-fat frozen entrees for healthier, more filling fast food.
- Add fresh spinach, sliced cucumber and zucchini, sprouts, and shredded carrots, to liven up your sandwich.
- Keep a pot of homemade vegetable soup on hand for a healthy, filling meal.
- Try different colored peppers in pasta for a delightful change of pace.
- Add vegetables and beans to your stews, soups, or pasta sauce.
- Reach for cut, raw vegetables kept crisp in water in the refrigerator.
- Try mashed cauliflower in place of mashed potatoes for variety.
- Marinate fresh vegetables like asparagus, sliced peppers, zucchini, and onions in a low fat dressing and grill or broil to serve as a gourmet side dish.
- Use leftover grilled vegetables on sandwiches, pizzas, and pastas.

Go for whole grains. When foods have been highly processed or refined, their fiber content may be reduced or even eliminated. Therefore, when choosing bread, crackers, pasta, rice, and cereals, check the food label for fiber content—the higher the better.

- Look for whole wheat, whole grain, or bran first in the ingredient list on bread and other grain products.

- High-fiber foods may have a coarser texture and are typically darker in color. However, don't be misled by dyes added by the manufacturer. Look at the nutrition label for the number of grams of fiber per serving.

- Try brown rice and whole wheat pastas. Many people say they really prefer the flavor and texture once they try them. You can mix them with the traditional white version for a while to get used to the difference.

- For variety, there are many exciting and flavorful grains available in the market. Look for wild rice, basmati rice, jasmine rice, barley, bulgur, couscous, quinoa, polenta, and kasha. Cook according to package directions or use vegetable or chicken broth in place of water. Add fresh or dried herbs, a small amount of olive oil, flavored vinegar, and diced vegetables for a hot side dish or cold salad.

- Replace part of the white flour with oat bran or wheat flour when baking.

It's not just the *what*, but the *how*. How carbohydrates are prepared and how they are served has a huge impact on their nutritional value. Sauces and condiments boost flavor and interest but be aware that they sometimes add significant calories and fat. Here are some practical tips:

- Substitute or use less sauce containing butter, cream, cheese, and oil.

- Choose red or tomato sauces in place of white or cream sauces on your pasta.

- Add bouillon cubes, broth, or minced garlic in place of butter or oil for an extra touch of flavor when preparing rice or mashed potatoes.

- Use fresh herbs, spice blends, seasoned vinegars, or lemon juice as flavorful seasonings.

- Top your toast, bread and bagels with all-fruit spreads, lower fat cream cheese, fancy mustards, and other low fat alternatives.

- Try low-fat or non-fat sour cream, non-fat ricotta, steamed vegetables, or good old salt and pepper in place of butter, sour cream, cheese, and bacon on baked potatoes.

- Fill a whole wheat tortilla with beans, grilled and fresh vegetables, lean meats, fish, or chicken, and fresh salsa— no need for sour cream or cheese here.

- Fresh sweet corn is delicious with a little salt and pepper—no butter needed.

Breakfast is a great time for a healthy dose of carbs. You have probably heard "breakfast is the most important meal of the day"—but that really depends on what you choose to eat.

- Choose whole-wheat bagels, toast, and English muffins instead of pastries, croissants, donuts, and muffins that contain less fiber and more fat. And don't forget to watch your portion sizes.

- Look for cereals with 5 or more grams of fiber per serving. If you aren't used to it, try mixing it with your usual cereal for a while.

- Top high-fiber cereal with fresh fruit, skim milk, or low-fat yogurt.

- Have a little peanut butter, egg white omelet, low-fat cheese, or other protein along with your carbohydrates to give you more sustained energy.

Dairy products have many benefits. In addition to being a source of carbohydrates in the form of lactose, dairy products also contain protein, calcium, and other important nutrients. In addition, studies have shown that those who consume 3-4 servings of dietary calcium daily in the form of milk, cheese, or yogurt had lower body fat percentages or gained less weight and body fat over time.

- Lower your saturated fat intake by drinking skim milk. If you are used to regular (full-fat or 4%) milk, cut back to 2%, then 1%, then skim (non-fat). You can even mix two types together to gradually adjust to the switch—for example, 2% and 1% to make 11/2%.

• There are many great lower fat versions of most dairy products. Experiment with different types and different brands to find the ones that balance good flavor with good health.

Health Notes: Trouble Digesting Dairy?

If you develop uncomfortable side effects such as diarrhea, cramps, gas, or bloating when you eat or drink dairy, you may be lactose intolerant. Lactose intolerance means that your intestines don't produce enough of the enzyme lactase to break down the amount of lactose you consume. The undigested lactose draws water into the colon causing diarrhea and cramps. In addition, intestinal bacteria break down the undigested milk sugars causing gas and bloating.

If you are lactose intolerant there are a few things you can do. Experiment with consuming dairy in small amounts. You may even be able to gradually increase the amount you can consume over time. Consume dairy with meals rather than by themselves. You may also find that you tolerate certain types of dairy products such as yogurt or cheese. Lactose-reduced or lactose-free milk is available or you can try lactase tablets, drops, and products supplemented with lactase to assist your digestion of dairy. If you can't or don't want to consume dairy products, you will need to increase you intake of other calcium containing foods and consider taking a calcium supplement (see Chapter 7).

Finally, what about sugar? Many people refer to sugar as empty calories. This is because it provides calories in the form of glucose without other nutrients like vitamins, minerals, or fiber. However, since it is a source of calories that can be used for energy and since it provides pleasure for those who like it, sugar is really not empty.

But some people believe that they are addicted to sugar. By addicted they usually mean that they crave sugar or feel out of control around it. This may happen when they eat sugary foods in response to emotional triggers. These feelings may also develop because sugar is often labeled as bad, so they have tried to resist their urges to eat it. If they eat it anyway, they may feel guilty and weak-willed.

Using an "all foods fit" approach, sugar is an acceptable source of energy as part of a balanced diet. Do keep in mind that if you eat an excessive amount of sugary foods, there won't be enough room in your diet for foods with other important nutrients. Once again, the keys are variety, balance, and moderation—and it is easier to practice moderation when you let go of the guilt about eating certain types of foods.

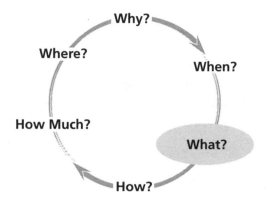

CHAPTER 5

Decision Point: What Will I Choose to Eat?

You've practiced identifying hunger and deciding *how* hungry you are. The next step in this system is to ask, "*What will I choose to eat?*" This step will help you make an optimal choice to satisfy your body and soul.

At this point, we could give you a list of allowed foods and portion sizes to choose from—but then you would be right back where you were on your last diet. Instead, think of Angie and Tom from Chapter 1, who eat instinctively. What would they do?

They would eat what they want.

You might be thinking, "That's fine for them since they are thin, but I only seem to want 'bad' food." However, remember that in this system, all foods fit—so you will actually get to make a choice about what you will eat. So how do you choose? Let's see what Angie does.

Angie ate her usual breakfast, fiber cereal with fruit and milk and a cup of coffee. She put a crockpot of beans on before she left the house and packed up the casserole she was taking to the office for their holiday potluck. She got hungry again mid-morning as she often does and decided to eat just half of one of the oranges that she keeps at her desk. At lunch, she surveyed the buffet table, and as usual, the staff brought all kinds of delicious foods to eat. There was a veggie platter with dip, chips and salsa, a colorful spinach salad, a crockpot of chili, two casseroles (including the one she brought), and two of her favorite desserts. She chose chips and salsa, spinach salad, a small amount of the casserole that someone else brought, and half of a serving of each of the desserts. She wasn't hungry for her usual afternoon snack that day so she was glad that the beans were ready when she got home.

Let's take a closer look at how and why Angie made those decisions. She has a weekday breakfast routine that she feels keeps her regular. She took a few minutes in the morning to start something for dinner so it would be ready when she got home. She always makes a point of having healthy food available at her desk to eat when she gets hungry, but that day she ate only half of her orange, wanting to be sure she was hungry for the potluck.

At the potluck, Angie didn't try to take a little of everything. Even though she loves vegetables and tries to eat plenty to keep her healthy, she didn't bother with the veggies and dip because she can get those anytime and she didn't want to be too full to try the desserts. She skipped the chili because she was already planning to have beans for dinner and too many make her feel bloated. The spinach salad was both healthy and delicious so that was an easy decision for her. She passed on her own casserole, knowing there would probably be leftovers that she could have for lunch the next day. She loves sweets so she was careful to save room for dessert.

Although Angie doesn't have to analyze each of her decisions, they can be summarized by three questions: "What do I want?" "What do I need?" "What do I have?" You can use these same questions to help you make food choices that are healthful and satisfying.

What Do I Want?

Often, when you are physically hungry, a specific food, flavor, or texture will come to mind. As you get used to listening to your body's signals, you will begin to recognize what type of food or taste will match your particular hunger at that time. Kim gave us a good example of why this is important:

> *I was hungry and I really wanted a few of the chocolate chip cookies that I had bought for my kids' lunches. I've been trying to lose weight so I decided to eat rice cakes instead. At first I felt good about it but I just didn't feel completely satisfied. I decided to eat some yogurt, then I ate some baby carrots, and then some cheese. I took a few bites out of the ice cream carton and then I finally gave in and had the chocolate chip cookies. I felt so guilty that I ended up eating almost half the package before my kids came home. Afterward I felt sick and I thought what did I accomplish here? It would have been better to eat a few chocolate chips cookies in the first place and really enjoy them while I was hungry.*

People often worry that if they ask themselves what they are really hungry for, they will always choose foods they "shouldn't." At first this might be true, since cravings tend to get stronger when you have been ignoring them. However, once you let go of the guilt about eating certain foods, you will find that you will want a variety of foods to feel healthy and satisfied. We will work on this more in a later chapter but the truth is, as you learn to listen to yourself, you will discover that your body has wisdom. Listen to what Gary had to say:

> *When you said "all foods fit" I was sure that all I would eat was steak and potatoes—and I did, for the first day and a half. But when I began asking myself what I really wanted, I found that I actually wanted salad*

sometimes. By the end of the week, I was eating chicken, trout, fruit, soup, and even quiche. It was great to see what my taste buds would come up with next.

The next time you are hungry, try to identify what you are hungry for. Ask yourself the following questions:

- What taste do I want—sweet, salty, sour, spicy, or bitter?
- What texture do I want—crunchy, creamy, smooth, or juicy?
- What temperature do I want—hot, moderate, cold, or frozen?
- What type of food do I want—light, heavy, or in-between?
- Do I want a certain category of food—such as protein, vegetables, or bread?
- Is there a specific food I have been craving?

If a particular food does not come to mind, simply choose a food that you usually enjoy and test a small amount to see if it is satisfying.

You will probably discover that you are often hungry for very specific flavors, textures, or types of foods. Initially, you may find that you want high fat or sugary foods more frequently, especially if you have been depriving yourself of these foods by dieting. Once those foods are not off-limits, you will notice that your body will crave healthier foods more often.

More importantly, you will see that matching the food you choose to what you are hungry for leads to greater satisfaction and more enjoyment—with less food.

What Do I Need?

Food decisions are not "good" or "bad" but clearly, some foods offer more nutritional benefits than others. As you consider what food to choose, ask yourself, "What does my body need?"

Keep in mind the principles of balance, variety and moderation. For instance, you could ask yourself questions like,

"Have I eaten a variety of fruits and vegetables today? Have I been eating a lot of junk food or fast food lately? Do I eat too much protein or not enough? Do I feel tired when I eat too many carbohydrates in one meal? What else might I be eating today?" Your answers to questions like these will help you decide which foods will best meet your nutritional needs.

To learn to balance eating for nutrition with eating for enjoyment, focus on the following strategies:

- Educate yourself about the nutritional aspects of food. Once you know how one food compares to another, you will often find yourself preferring the more nutritious food. The nutrition section in each chapter of *Am I Hungry?* provides the information you need to make healthy choices.

- Know your personal nutrition needs based on your health. For example, a history of high cholesterol or a family history of diabetes will affect your nutritional needs. Talk to your doctor or a dietitian for specific recommendations.

- Keep in mind the principles of variety, balance, and moderation when you ask yourself, "What do I need?"

- Remember that small changes really do make a difference and healthy eating is simply the result of all the positive decisions you make.

- Be willing to try new foods—you just might surprise yourself. However, don't persist in making yourself eat foods that you just don't like.

- Enjoy your healthy choices by focusing on fresh foods, appealing combinations, new flavors, and interesting recipes.

- Make it a habit to choose more healthful foods unless you feel that you really need to eat a particular food to feel satisfied.

- Always ask yourself, "Is there a healthy choice that will meet my needs without feeling deprived?" For instance, could you be happy with frozen yogurt instead of ice cream this time?

What Do I Have?

This step can be summarized with one word: planning. Having a variety of foods available is very important if you are going to learn to use hunger to guide your eating. If you feel hungry and the only thing available is a vending machine, you are likely to choose a snack food that may not be very healthy, may not taste very good, and may not really be what you were hungry for anyway. Notice that Angie had the ingredients for the breakfast she enjoys, she started dinner before she left for work, and she kept fruit at her desk to eat when she was hungry.

The key is to keep a variety of foods available that are appealing but not overly tempting. These are foods that you enjoy when you are hungry but won't be calling out to you from their storage place saying, "Come eat me!" If you are finding certain foods too challenging for you to stop eating even when you are comfortably satiated, you may want to introduce those more slowly.

Stock your home, workplace, and even your car, purse or briefcase with different types of foods—including healthful options—that meet many of the types of cravings you get. You will always have something available that will be satisfying. Margo had a great idea:

> *I used to eat out for lunch nearly every day, mostly because it was convenient. I knew I was spending a lot of money and I wasn't making the best choices for my health so I decided to start taking my lunch to work. At the beginning of the week, I bring a small grocery bag full of lunch items like soup, lunchmeat and rolls, frozen dinners, pretzels, yogurt, fruit, veggies, and even a few snack size candy bars. Now, no matter what I'm in the mood for, I can find something satisfying and I am not as tempted to run out for a burger and fries.*

Putting It All Together

To summarize, once you have decided that you are hungry enough to eat, you will need to choose food. Ask yourself, "What do I want?" Decide if there is a particular food or type of food that you are hungry for. Keep in mind that there are no forbidden foods.

Next ask, "What do I need?" Take a brief inventory of what you have been eating or what you will be eating that day and see if there is something that your body needs that you should consider when making your choice. Think variety, balance, and moderation, and make the healthiest choice possible that will not leave you feeling deprived.

Finally ask, "What do I have?" Consider the available options and choose something based on what you are hungry for and what your body needs. It really helps if you are prepared for hunger at all times—so make a point of having healthy, satisfying choices with you wherever you go. Of course, like Angie at her potluck, you are not always in control of which foods are offered. In that case, simply look at what is available then make your best possible choice.

If you are not used to choosing food in this manner, you may find it challenging at first. However, these steps allow you to balance eating for pleasure with eating for health. With practice, making optimal choices for yourself becomes easier and more automatic. Eating food that you truly enjoy while taking good care of your body is just another way you can begin to move toward optimal health.

Fitness: Essentials of Flexibility

Flexibility is a key part of a complete and balanced fitness program. Flexibility is the ability of your joints to move through their full range of motion. Stretching exercises increase your flexibility by using gentle, stretching movements to increase the length of your muscles and connective tissues around your joints. Improving your flexibility by stretching regularly will decrease muscular tension and stiffness, help reduce your risk of injury, and maintain your body's mobility and freedom of movement in daily life.

Stretching feels good. Animals (including humans) stretch instinctively. Observe a cat or a dog stretch spontaneously, almost lazily—naturally tuning up all of their muscles. Infants will arch their back and stretch their arms when picked up after a nap. After sitting in one position too long, people naturally stretch to relieve stiffness. If this spontaneous stretching can feel this good, imagine how good it will feel to stretch all of your muscles regularly as part of your overall fitness program.

Benefits of Stretching

Increased flexibility has many benefits:

• Decreases the tension and stiffness in your muscles.

• Maintains and increases the range of motion in your joints by increasing the length of your muscles and tendons.

• Promotes blood flow and nutrient supply to your muscles and surrounding tissues.

• Enhances muscular relaxation. Stretched muscles hold less tension, which may help reduce stress.

• Optimizes functional movement in your daily life.

- Offsets age-related stiffness and may slow the degeneration of the joints.

- Reduces your risk of injury. Stretching improves elasticity so your muscles and joints are able to move further before an injury occurs.

- Helps you develop body awareness and improved coordination.

- Prepares your body for exercise. Stretching after you warm up, prior to more vigorous exercise, allows the muscles to loosen and respond more efficiently during your activities.

- Reduces muscle soreness after you exercise. Many exercises tighten and shorten your muscles. Stretching afterwards will lengthen those muscles again, which may lessen those aches and pains.

- Improves your athletic performance and efficiency. By increasing your joint range of motion, you will decrease the resistance in your muscles during various activities.

- Improves your posture and muscular balance. Stretching the muscles of the lower back, shoulders and chest will help keep your back in better alignment and improve your posture.

- Decreases your risk of lower back pain. Improved flexibility in the hamstrings, hip flexors, quadriceps, and other muscles attached to the pelvis will relieve tension on the lumbar spine and reduce the risk of lower back pain.

- Makes you feel good!

What You Need to Know

Everybody benefits from stretching. The methods are gentle, easy, and apply regardless of age, natural flexibility, or fitness level. You do not have to get into shape to stretch but even athletes rely on flexibility training for peak performance. Consult with your doctor if you've been sedentary or have had any recent physical problems before beginning any exercise program.

The best time to stretch is when the muscle is warm. Like taffy, a warm muscle is more elastic and relaxes more easily. Over-stretching a cold muscle can cause injury. Therefore, if you are going to stretch before exercise, warm up first by walking or doing your planned cardiorespiratory activity at a light intensity for 5 to 10 minutes. This will increase the elasticity and circulation to the muscles. Remember, stretching is *not* the same thing as warming up.

Before Exercise: When you stretch before your workout (but after your warm up, of course), gently stretch all of the muscles you'll be using. For example, if you are going to ride a bike, lightly stretch the muscles in the front and back of your thighs and your lower legs.

During Exercise: Take a moment to stretch during cardiorespiratory activities when you stop to rest or take a drink. While strength training, you can stretch the muscles you are using between each set. We will address this further in the next chapter.

After Exercise: An important time to stretch is after you finish exercising. This will lengthen your muscles again and release the tightness that exercise may produce. Be sure to stretch all of the muscles you used during your work out.

Anytime: Gentle stretching can be done anytime you feel like it: in the morning to begin your day, while sitting in a car, at your desk, after a warm bath or shower, or while you are just relaxing. Stretching is beneficial whenever you feel muscular stiffness or need to release nervous tension. A few minutes a day of gentle stretching can relax your body *and* your mind.

Getting Started

Stretching feels good when it is done correctly. It is very important to listen to your body during stretching. You should not experience any pain when you are stretching properly. Stretching should be peaceful, relaxing, and non-competitive. There are numerous methods for stretching specific muscles but here are a few common basics.

- **Warm Up:** Always make sure your muscles are warm before stretching, for example, by walking at a comfortable pace for 5 to 10 minutes.

- **Breathe:** Exhale as you begin the stretch. Continue to take slow, rhythmical breaths throughout the stretch. Do not hold your breath.

- **Listen to your body:** Start by slowly stretching to the point of mild, comfortable tension. Do not stretch to the point of pain.

- **Relax: Relax as you hold the stretch.** The feeling of tension should subside as you hold the position. If it does not, ease off slightly and find a degree of tension that is comfortable. As you inhale, release the stretch slightly and as you exhale relax further into the stretch.

- **Hold:** Hold the stretch for 10 to 30 seconds. As you feel the tension decrease, you can increase the stretch until you feel a slight pull again.

- **No bouncing!** Bouncing activates the stretch reflex that causes tightening of the muscles so it is counterproductive.

- **Repeat:** When time allows, repeat each stretch two or three times for optimal benefit.

Get FITT

Frequency: The American College of Sports Medicine recommends that you stretch at least two to three times per week.

Intensity: Stretching should always be gentle and relaxed. Stretch to the point of comfortable tension.

Time: The length of the entire stretching session can be as little as 15 seconds or as long as 20 minutes, depending on the number of muscles you want to stretch and the number of times you stretch each muscle. When you first start working on your flexibility, hold each stretch for 10 seconds. With time and practice, try to increase the time your hold each stretch to 30 seconds. For optimal benefit, repeat each stretch three or four times.

Type: Do post-exercise stretching and head-to-toe stretching at home using the suggestions below. Try stretch classes, yoga, and Pilates at a gym or on video.

Stretch Yourself

Use the flexibility exercises below to stretch the specific muscle you have used during a cardiorespiratory or strength training session. For example, after a walk, cycling, or a lower body strength training session, do the lower back and leg stretches. After swimming, tennis, or an upper body strength training, do arm, chest, and upper back stretches. By doing the entire sequence, these flexibility exercises will provide a good head-to-toe stretching session.

Neck Stretch

Muscles: The neck and upper back (trapezius) muscles.

Relax your neck muscles and bend your head forward to touch your chin on your chest. Hold for 10 to 30 seconds. Lean your head back and hold. Lift your head again and place one hand on the side of your head. Slowly lean your head to the side then use your hand to gently stretch the neck muscles. Repeat on the opposite side.

Shoulder Stretch

Muscles: The shoulders and upper back.

Reach your right arm out in front of your body. Place your left wrist on your right elbow and pull your right arm across your chest. Keeping your right arm extended, use your left wrist to gently pull your right arm as close to your body as possible. Hold for 10 to 30 seconds. Repeat on the opposite side.

Triceps Stretch

Muscles: The triceps (located on the back of your upper arm) and shoulders.

Raise your right arm toward the ceiling then bend your elbow and touch your neck or upper back with the palm of your right hand so that your right elbow points to the ceiling. Grasp your right elbow with your left hand and pull it gently to the left until you feel a stretching sensation at the back of your upper right arm. Hold for 10 to 30 seconds. Repeat on the opposite side.

Cat Stretch

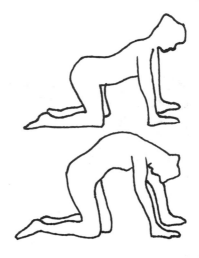

Muscles: The entire back including the cervical, thoracic, and lumbar spine.

Position yourself comfortably on your hands and knees with your back level. Inhale as you lift your head and allow your back to sag. Slowly exhale as you contract your stomach muscles and curve your back upward toward the ceiling, allowing your head to drop down and your tail to curve in. Hold for 10 to 30 seconds. Inhale as you slowly return to the starting position. Exhale then repeat.

Lower Back Extension Stretch

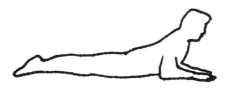

Muscles: The abdominal and supporting muscles of the lower back (lumbar spine).

Lie on your stomach and extend your arms slightly in front of you with your elbows positioned under your shoulders. Gently raise your head and chest off the floor, leaning comfortably on your forearms. You should feel this stretch in your lower back and along the front of your body. Hold for 10 to 30 seconds.

Lower Back Flexion Stretch

Muscles: The supporting muscles of the lower back (lumbar spine).

Lie on your back with both legs extended straight out. Bend your right knee and clasp it with both hands, then slowly pull the knee toward your chest. Hold for 10 to 30 seconds then switch legs. Alternatively, you can pull both knees in at the same time.

Spinal Twist

Muscles: The entire back and the sides of your trunk.

While seated, extend your right leg in front of you. Bend your left leg and place your left foot on the outside of the right knee. Extend your left arm behind you and place your left palm on the floor to support your body. Use your right arm to gently twist your torso to the left until you feel the stretch along your right side and back. Hold for 10 to 30 seconds. Repeat on the opposite side.

Inner Thigh Stretch

Muscles: The inner thigh and groin muscles.

While seated, pull both feet inward toward your body. Grasp your feet with your hands and press down slightly on your knees with your elbows. Hold for 10 to 30 seconds. Repeat on opposite side.

Hamstring Stretch

Muscles: The hamstrings, located in the back of the upper legs.

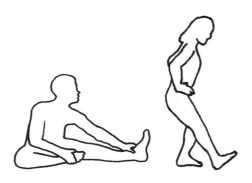

Sitting: Sit comfortably on the floor with your right leg straight and your left leg bent, so that the sole of your left foot rests flat against the inside of your right leg. While keeping your lower back straight, slowly reach toward your right foot until you feel a gentle stretching sensation in your right hamstring. During this stretch, keep your right foot pointing upward. Hold for 10 to 30 seconds. Repeat on the opposite side.

Standing: Place your right foot about 12 inches in front of the left foot. Lift the ball of the right foot and keep your leg straight. Bend the back leg and lean forward into the front leg. Place your hands on your right thigh for balance. Hold for 10 to 30 seconds. Repeat on the opposite side.

Chest Stretch

Muscles: The chest, shoulders, and back.

Lace your fingers behind your back so that your palms are facing in toward your spine, thumbs pointing down at the ground. Hold your chin up and lift your chest as high as you can. Pull your shoulders back and lower your linked hands down slightly toward the ground. Hold for 10 to 30 seconds. Release the tension and relax for a few seconds. Now slowly raise your linked hands up toward the ceiling, keeping your neck and back relaxed until you feel a gentle stretching sensation in the front of your chest and shoulders.

Calf Stretch

Muscles: The calf muscles, located at the back of the lower leg.

While standing, place your hands or forearms on a wall. Place your right foot near the wall and keeping your left foot flat on the floor, move your left leg back until you feel the stretch in the left calf muscle and the back of your ankle (Achilles tendon). Hold for 10 to 30 seconds. Repeat on the opposite side.

Quadriceps Stretch

Muscles: The quadriceps (quads), located in the front of the upper legs (thighs).

Stand tall and support your body with your right hand against a wall or solid object for balance. Raise your right heel toward your buttocks then grasp your toes or ankle with your left hand. Gently pull your heel up to your buttocks until you feel the stretch in your thigh. Hold for 10 to 30 seconds. Repeat on opposite the side.

Modification: If you are unable to reach your toes or ankle, pull on your pant leg to raise your foot. Alternatively, you can place your ankle on the seat of a chair placed behind you if that is enough of a stretch for the front of your thigh.

Keep It Interesting

- As with any exercise, varying your flexibility program will help you stick with it.

- In addition to stretching after exercise, periodically set aside time for a head-to-toe stretch session. It feels so good.

- Listening to music and focusing on your breath can help you relax. When you are relaxed, your body is more responsive to flexibility training.

- Use towels, straps, large balls, and other accessories to add diversity and effectiveness to your stretching.

- Try a stretching class. These are available on video or DVD or may be offered by your local fitness facility, community center, or community college. Some focus exclusively on flexibility while others combine cardiorespiratory and strength training with stretching.

- Yoga and Pilates are great additions to your regular fitness program. They will increase your flexibility and strength while teaching you to relax and calm your mind.

Stretching regularly is a wonderful way to relax while you build your flexibility. It will help you tune-up while you tune-in to your body.

Nutrition: Essentials of Fat

There have been numerous studies and reports concerning fat and fat intake, sometimes offering confusing or conflicting recommendations. There is ongoing research; here is a summary of what you need to know to make the best choices.

The Role of Fat in Your Health

Fat is a chemical compound made of fatty acids. Fat has many important roles. Not only is fat the main storage form of energy, but it is necessary for normal body function. Dietary fat (the fat in your diet) is needed to promote growth and development (especially brain development during childhood), maintain healthy skin and hair, and help transport and absorb certain vitamins (A, D, E, and K). Importantly, fats also provide flavor and texture to the foods you eat and satisfaction from your meals.

One gram of dietary fat provides your body with 9 calories to store or use as energy. For comparison, one gram of protein or carbohydrates each have 4 calories. Therefore, the calorie content of fat is over twice as high, which may make it easier to consume too many calories when eating high fat foods. Furthermore, since dietary fat is already in the chemical storage form your body prefers, your body is able to store any excess easily as body fat. However, it is very important to recognize that an excess intake of calories from *any* source will be converted to body fat for storage.

While eating too much dietary fat (or too much of any macronutrient) can contribute to excess calorie intake, excessive intake of fat, particularly certain types of fat is associated with heart disease, cancer, and other medical problems. Once again, knowledge about nutrition will help you make the best choices for your body.

The Many Faces of Fats

The two main types of fat are saturated and unsaturated (named for their chemical bonds). Unsaturated fats are either monounsaturated or polyunsaturated. The fats in food are actually made up of a mixture of these three different types of fatty acids (saturated, monounsaturated, polyunsaturated) and are named by the fatty acid they have the most of. They are different types of fats that have different effects on your health.

Saturated fat is typically solid at room temperature. Saturated fats raise blood cholesterol, which increases the risk of heart disease. Therefore, it is recommended that no more than 10 percent of your total daily calories come from saturated fats.

Saturated fat is found in animal products including meat and meat products, dairy products, egg yolks, and butter. Tropical oils like palm, palm kernel, and coconut oils are also saturated and are typically found in candy, snack products, and movie popcorn.

Unsaturated fat is liquid at room temperature. It typically comes from plant products and fish. There are two types of naturally occurring unsaturated fats: polyunsaturated and monounsaturated.

- **Polyunsaturated fat** is a healthier alternative to saturated fat because it decreases total cholesterol. It is primarily found in these oils: safflower, sunflower, corn, sesame seed, flaxseed, soybean, and cottonseed. Fish is also an excellent source.

- **Monounsaturated fat** helps lower cholesterol when eaten in place of saturated fat. Good sources include canola oil, olive oil, and peanut oil. A helpful way to remember these is the acronym COP (Canola, Olive, Peanut). Avocado, nuts, olives, and peanut butter also contain monounsaturated fats.

Trans Fat: A fourth type of fat, called trans fat, is a result of man-made processes that alter unsaturated fats. Food manufacturers make trans fat by bubbling hydrogen gas into liquid vegetable oils. These oils become partially hydrogenated which make them more solid. This process causes healthier unsaturated fats to become less healthy fats that raise the risk of heart disease. They are often found in margarine, shortening, chips, snack foods, crackers, baked goods, and fried foods. Until they are listed separately on the food label, look for the words hydrogenated or partially hydrogenated in the ingredient list. The closer to the beginning of the list it appears, the more of it the product contains.

Fats at a Glance

Types	Effects on Health	Subtypes	Examples	Typical Serving Sizes (Based on 5 grams of fat)
Saturated Fats (Solid)	Raise cholesterol		Butter Lard Palm oil Palm kernel oil Coconut oil Cocoa Butter	1 teaspoon
			Cream cheese Cream Half & half Sour cream Mayonnaise Cream-based salad dressings	1 tablespoon 2 tablespoons 2 tablespoons 2 tablespoons 1 teaspoon 1 tablespoon
			Fatty meats Egg yolks Dairy products	Varies
Unsaturated Fats (Liquid)	Lower cholesterol	Polyunsaturated	Margarine Safflower oil Sunflower oil Corn oil Sesame seed oil Flaxseed oil Soybean oil Cottonseed oil	1 teaspoon
			Oil-based salad dressings	1 tablespoon
			Fish	Varies
		Monounsaturated	Canola oil Olive oil Peanut oil	1 teaspoon
			Avocado Nuts Olives Peanut butter	1/5 of whole 1 oz., 1/3 cup 11 large 1/2 tablespoon

Health Notes: Cholesterol and Heart Disease

There are many known risk factors for heart disease including smoking, high blood pressure, diabetes, family history, obesity, physical inactivity, and high cholesterol.

Cholesterol is not actually a fatty acid but it is a cousin of fat in the lipid family. Cholesterol plays an important functional role in your body—but too much cholesterol can lead to heart disease. Cholesterol comes from two sources: it is *made* in your liver and it is *consumed* in your diet. Your cholesterol levels are partly hereditary and partly dietary.

Your liver manufactures cholesterol because it is necessary for building cell membranes and nerve tissue, helping produce necessary hormones for body regulation, and producing bile acids for digestion. Other animals manufacture cholesterol for these same reasons; therefore, dietary cholesterol is found in the animal products you may eat, such as meat, poultry, egg yolks, cheese, whole milk, and other whole-milk dairy products.

Some people manufacture the right amount of cholesterol but eat too much cholesterol and saturated fat in their diet, raising their blood cholesterol levels and putting themselves at increased risk of heart disease. For others, high cholesterol levels and heart disease run in their family; their body may be genetically programmed to manufacture too much cholesterol.

Knowing your cholesterol level is important for determining if you are at increased risk of heart disease. However, the total cholesterol doesn't tell the whole story. Cholesterol is transported in different forms, which have different effects:

LDL: Low-density lipoproteins (LDL) are considered "bad" because they are sticky and likely to form fatty deposits and plaque on the walls of your arteries leading to blockage. For a healthy person, an LDL level of less than 130 mg/dl is desirable. A person with other risk factors such as a history of heart disease or diabetes should maintain an LDL level of less than 100 mg/dl. Eating polyunsaturated and monounsaturated fats (olive, peanut, and canola oil) may help lower your LDL levels. Remember: L̲DL = The L̲ower the better.

HDL: High-density lipoproteins (HDL) are considered "good" because they help carry away cholesterol that is stuck to the walls of the arteries. A high level of HDL is associated with a lower incidence of heart disease. An HDL level of more than 40 mg/dl is optimal. Regular physical activity and exercise can raise your levels of this "good" cholesterol. Remember: H̲DL = The H̲igher the better.

Triglycerides: Triglycerides are another form in which fat is transported through the blood. Triglyceride levels below 150 mg/dl are considered normal according to the National Heart, Lung, and Blood Institute. Higher levels can be the result of eating high fat foods, drinking alcohol in excess, diabetes, inherited disorders, and pancreatic disorders. Very high levels can have serious medical complications.

If you have a personal or family history of elevated cholesterol levels, heart disease, or diabetes, you will want to be even more cautious about eating high cholesterol foods and saturated fats. If necessary, consultation with a dietitian may help you determine how to change your diet. If your cholesterol remains high despite a careful low cholesterol diet and exercise, medications may be necessary to lower your cholesterol to safe levels. Discuss this with your doctor.

Getting the Most from Fats

Numerous health authorities recommend that your total fat intake should be in the range of 20 percent to 35 percent of your total calories. For example, a person requiring 2000 calories a day and striving for 30 percent of calories from fat, 600 calories or less of their daily intake should be from fat (approximately 65 grams or less). It is also recommended that 10 percent or less of your calories come from saturated fat and trans fat combined. Your cholesterol intake should be less than 300 milligrams daily.

Remember balance, variety, and moderation. By balancing your intake of higher fat foods with lower fat foods in the same meal or throughout the day, it is possible to stay within the total daily healthy fat guidelines while still enjoying flavorful foods. Eat a variety of foods that use the healthy oils and try a variety of preparation methods, for example grilled instead of fried, or roasted instead sautéed, to boost your health without sacrificing flavor. Learn to enjoy fat in moderation instead of all or nothing. Here are some key points:

Decrease your intake of saturated fat. It helps to remember this simple phrase: Saturated fat is Solid at room temperature and Sits in your arteries!

- Use healthier unsaturated fat instead of unhealthy saturated fat by choosing liquid fat instead of solid fat whenever possible.

- Cut back on animal products such as red meat, poultry with skin, eggs, whole fat dairy, and butter.

- Select leaner cuts of beef, pork, and poultry.

- Choose ground beef that is labeled lean. Drain excess fat carefully before adding additional ingredients. Less lean cuts of ground meat can be rinsed with hot water in a colander to remove excess fat after cooking.

- Trim the visible fat from meat.

- Remove the skin from chicken before cooking.

- Chill soups and stews made with poultry or meat and skim off the solidified fat before reheating to serve.

- Eat fish instead of meat twice a week.

- Have meatless meals regularly.

- Use low- or non-fat (skim) versions of your favorite dairy products.

- Limit snack foods made with tropical oils.

Watch your portion sizes of fat. Too much will make it more difficult to manage your weight and maximize your health. Look for ways to decrease your portion sizes, for example:

- Use less butter, oil, mayonnaise, cream cheese or other condiments.

- Use less than the usual amount of salad dressing, sauces, and toppings.
- Ask for your salad dressing and sauces on the side. Dip the tip of the tines of you fork in the dressing before you spear your salad; you will get a little flavor with every bite—but a lot less than you would if it was poured on.
- Spray your pans with cooking spray instead of coating them with fats and oils.
- Use less fat than a recipe calls for. This is more challenging with baking but it is possible to substitute applesauce or pureed prunes in some recipes.
- Use lower fat versions of your favorite foods. Be sure to read the label though; low fat doesn't necessarily mean low calorie.

Eat more fish. The omega-3 fatty acids in fish oil decrease the risk of sudden cardiac death and overall mortality.

- Try to eat at least two servings of fish each week. (If you have a history of coronary heart disease, the American Heart Association recommends one serving of fish daily).
- Fatty fish such as salmon and tuna have the highest levels of omega-3 fatty acids.
- If you don't like fish, consider taking fish oil capsules (one gram daily).
- Flaxseed, canola oil, and walnuts are also great sources of omega-3 fatty acids.

Watch trans fats. Look for the words hydrogenated or partially hydrogenated in the ingredient list—especially in snack foods and baked goods. Ask what kind of oil is used at your favorite restaurants.

Make healthy substitutions. There are many ways to decrease overall fat intake, particularly saturated and trans fats. The chart on the next page has many practical and delicious ideas.

Fat is an important nutrient. Not only is it a critical substance in your body, it also adds flavor and texture to your food. Identifying your personal health issues and learning about fats will allow you to make the best possible choice.

Fat: Making Healthier Choices

A HEALTHIER CHOICE:	INSTEAD OF:

Fats and Oils

Soft tub margarine made with safflower, corn, or sunflower oil	Butter or stick margarine made with partially hydrogenated oil
Canola, olive, or peanut oil	Lard, shortening, meat fat, coconut or palm oil
Nonstick pans or cooking spray	Cooking with butter or oil
Flavored vinegar or salad dressing made with oil	Regular salad dressing made with tropical oils, cream, or cheese
Dressing and sauces on the side	Served generously over the top
Broth	Butter or margarine
Mustard	Mayonnaise
Baked potato with low fat toppings	French Fries

Proteins

Grilled, broiled, boiled, baked	Fried
Skinless chicken or turkey	Poultry with skin
White meat poultry	Dark meat
Lean beef trimmed of visible fat	Prime, heavily marbled cuts, organ meats
Lean ground beef or turkey	Regular ground beef
Lean pork (loin, shoulder, leg)	Pork ribs or roast, hot dogs, bacon, sausage
Egg whites (2)	Whole egg
Low-fat egg substitute	Eggs
Low-fat varieties of fish	Shellfish
Meatless: beans, tofu	High-fat protein sources

Breads and Cereals

Bread, bagels, English muffins	Doughnuts, pastries, croissants
Rice and pasta with low fat toppings	Fried rice, crispy noodles, cream/butter sauces
Low fat hot or cold cereals	Granola

Dairy Products

Skim or 1% milk	Whole milk
Evaporated skim milk	Cream or half and half
Reduced or fat-free sour cream, cream cheese, yogurt	Regular sour cream, cream cheese, yogurt
Low-fat cheeses (skim mozzarella, cottage cheese, or ricotta cheese)	American, cheddar, Swiss, brie, other high-fat cheese
Frozen yogurt, ice milk, sherbet	Ice cream, shakes

Snacks and Desserts

Pretzels, light popcorn, flatbread crackers, melba toast, nuts (in moderation)	Chips, high-fat or fried snack foods, crackers made with butter, cheese, partially hydrogenated oils
Angel food cake, graham crackers, fruit, gingersnaps, cookies, real fruit popsicles, sherbet	High-fat cakes, cookies, candy, chocolate, desserts

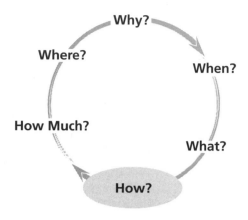

CHAPTER 6

Decision Point: How Will I Eat?

You are now more aware about the decisions you need to make about why and what you eat. Now, you will decide *how* you will eat.

Eating is a natural, healthy, and pleasurable activity when it is done to satisfy hunger. Choosing to eat mindfully, in other words, giving food and eating your full attention, will allow you to have optimal enjoyment and satisfaction from eating.

When you pay attention to your body's signals and savor your food, you feel satisfied with smaller quantities without feeling deprived. It is possible to truly enjoy food yet not eat to excess.

Mindful eating also allows you to experience the difference between physical *satisfaction* and *fullness*. When you eat on autopilot, you may only become aware when you are overly full. But at comfortable satiety—a 5 or 6 on the Hunger and Fullness Scale—your stomach may only be slightly distended. At that point, you *could* eat more food but your body is not asking for it. It is a very subtle feeling of stomach fullness (less obvious than the signal to start eating) so you must listen to your body carefully or you will miss it. This is where mindful eating comes in.

Another benefit to mindful eating is that you will notice how you feel, both physically and emotionally when you eat certain foods, eat in certain environments, or eat in certain ways. This may affect your future choices about eating. However, it is important to observe your eating from a *neutral* perspective. In other words, don't judge or punish yourself for the way you eat. Instead, learn from your heightened awareness to increase your satisfaction from food. Here is how Donna explained it:

I always said I couldn't lose weight because I love food and eating too much. But as I look back on my eating, I can't see how I could have really. I can remember so many times that I ate dinner while I was watching television and the next day I could barely remember what I ate—much less how it tasted. I would finish off a large bucket of popcorn at the movies but I would want just one more bite when it was gone because I didn't even realize I had eaten it. Sometimes I would eat something that tasted fantastic so I kept eating it. I don't think I really even tasted it after the first few bites. I think my mission was to finish it, not enjoy it. If I ate a really great meal I would usually ruin it by being so full when I was done that I felt miserable and guilty.

When I decided to start paying more attention to how I ate, I discovered a whole new world. I realized that some of the foods I used to eat all of the time don't really taste that great. Now I love to try new foods, new flavors, and new combinations. We go to new restaurants as much to experience the ambience as to eat the food. Eating has become a sensual experience for me. And surprisingly, I don't eat nearly as much as I did before—I just don't need to.

Strategies for Mindful Eating

Try these techniques to help you identify your body's signals and truly enjoy your food:

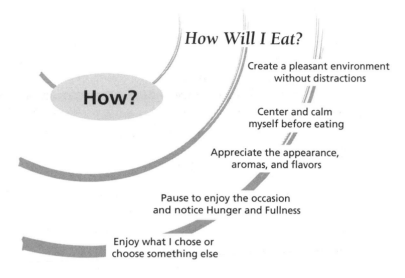

How Will I Eat?

How?

Create a pleasant environment without distractions

Center and calm myself before eating

Appreciate the appearance, aromas, and flavors

Pause to enjoy the occasion and notice Hunger and Fullness

Enjoy what I chose or choose something else

- **Get into the habit of checking in with yourself several times a day to see where you are on the Hunger and Fullness Scale.** Begin eating when you feel hungry, but don't wait until you're famished. One of the keys to conscious eating is to keep your body adequately fed to avoid becoming *overly* hungry which just increases the chance that you will overeat.

- **Decide how full you want to be at the end of eating.** If you don't have a plan, you are more likely to eat more than you needed or wanted to. For example, if you are really working on losing weight, you may decide that you will definitely stop at a 5. On the other hand, if it is a special occasion or special food, you may decide that it is worth being a little uncomfortable afterward so you plan to stop at a 7. Remember, you are in charge of how much you will eat.

- **Choose food that will satisfy both your body and your mind.** This is contrary to most of the usual diet rules so it takes some practice. To get the optimum level of satisfaction from your food and therefore eat less, remember to ask yourself : What do I want? What do I need? What do I have?

- **Purchase or prepare only the amount of food you think you will need.** With practice, you will be able to predict how much food it will take to fill you up at different levels of hunger.

- **Set the table in a pleasant manner.** Creating a pleasant ambience adds to the enjoyment of eating and to your level of satisfaction. Even when you are preparing food for yourself, make an effort to make it attractive as if you were serving it to someone special. (You are!)

- **Eat in a calm environment.** If you are upset or anxious about something, take some time to calm down before you begin eating. Likewise, don't eat while having stressful interactions with others.

- **Eat without distractions.** If you eat while you are distracted by watching television or talking on the telephone, you will not be giving your food or your body's signals your full attention Consequently, you may feel full after eating, but not satisfied. For example, do not eat while watching television, working, or driving.

- **Eat when you are sitting down.** Choose one or two particular areas at home and at work that are only used for eating and eat only there. For example, do not eat while standing over the sink, peering into the refrigerator, or sitting in bed.

- **Take a few breaths and center yourself before you begin eating.** This will help you slow down and give eating your full attention.

- **Appreciate the aroma and the appearance of your food.** Notice the colors, textures, and smells of the food and imagine what it will taste like.

- **Decide which food looks the most appetizing and start eating that food first.** If you save the best until last, you may want to eat it even if you are full.

- **Savor the aromas and tastes of your food as you eat it.** Put your fork down between bites and be conscious of all the different sensations you are experiencing.

- **Appreciate the occasion.** Appreciate the atmosphere, the company, or simply the fact that you are giving yourself the opportunity to sit down and enjoy your meal.

- **If you notice that you are not enjoying what you chose, choose something else if possible.** Eating food you do not enjoy will leave you feeling dissatisfied.

- **Pause in the middle of eating for at least two full minutes.** Ask yourself where you are on the Hunger and Fullness Scale. Estimate how much more food it will take to fill you to comfortable satiety.

- **Notice when your taste buds become less sensitive to the taste of food.** When the food doesn't taste as good as when you started eating, it's a sign that your body has had enough.

- **Push your plate forward or get up from the table as soon as you feel satisfied.** The desire to keep eating will pass quickly. Keep in mind that you'll eat again when you are hungry.

- **When you finish eating ask yourself where you are on the Hunger and Fullness Scale.** If you overate, don't punish yourself. Just notice the physical and/or emotional discomfort that often accompanies being overly full and create a plan to decrease the likelihood that you will overeat next time.

Mindful eating will make it possible for you to experience the difference between physical satisfaction and fullness. Since this feeling is very subtle, you must listen carefully to your body's signals or you will miss it. Mindful eating also allows you to feel more satisfied with smaller quantities of food. Learning to savor your food simply makes eating more pleasurable.

As with the other strategies you have learned in this book, learning to eat mindfully takes practice. Set aside time each day to walk through this process until it becomes natural for you. Look at what happened when Marcia tried it:

"I love to munch on sweets or salty, crunchy snacks like chips or pretzels while I read. At first they taste really good, but then I get involved in the story and the next thing I know, I've eaten the whole bag. I feel so full but I swear, I can't remember eating them all! I think I eat on autopilot and I don't stop until the book ends, the food is gone, or I realize that I am totally stuffed.

Well, chocolate is absolutely my favorite food. A good friend of mine brought a small box of truffles home for me from her trip to Europe. I was about to pop one into my mouth while I was reading when I thought, if I love them that much, don't they deserve my undivided attention? I waited until I was hungry and really wanted one of those truffles. You'll probably think I'm silly, but I put the truffle on a china plate, cut it into eight little pieces and sat in my dining room, savoring every little morsel. It was rich and creamy and absolutely wonderful. I think the only thing that could have made it any better would have been eating it in Belgium!"

Mindful Eating Strategies for the Real World

It is easier to become distracted from signals of physical hunger and satiety at restaurants and social gatherings, especially when food is treated as the main event. Furthermore, eating mindfully in the workplace poses some common challenges. In these environments, you will need to pay extra close attention to your body's signals.

- It's common to have dishes of candy or snacks set out at parties and in many places of business. Avoid indulging in food just because it's there. Grazing in an unconscious manner can lead to many extra calories that you may not even remember enjoying.

- Since the duration of the meals tends to be extended at social events, you may need to have your plate taken away (or put your napkin on it) once you are satisfied, to avoid nibbling unconsciously.

- Be aware of the effects of alcohol on the mindful eating process.

- Before having one of those doughnuts, bagels or brownies that were brought in to the break room at work, check your hunger scale. If you are hungry and you wish to choose that particular food to satisfy you, remember to sit down and eat it consciously. If you are not hungry, save some of the food for later or skip it altogether—it is likely that food will reappear another day.

- Don't eat at your desk or while conducting business. Make enough time to enjoy a meal without work interruptions if possible. Even during business lunches or dinners make it a point to alternately focus on the business at hand then on your food and eating.

This process may feel awkward at first, especially if you are used to eating on autopilot. But by choosing to eat mindfully, you will probably find yourself losing weight while experiencing *more* pleasure and satisfaction from your food than you *ever* did while dieting. Knowing what satisfies you and getting the most pleasure from your eating experiences are key factors for a lifetime of weight control.

Once you have experienced the increased pleasure from eating mindfully, you may be motivated to become more mindful during other activities too. Living in the moment and becoming more aware can increase your enjoyment and effectiveness in everything you do.

Fitness: Essentials of Strength Training

Strength training is the third component of fitness—last but certainly not least. Strength training will help you function optimally in your daily life and increase your metabolism. Fortunately, you can maintain and even gain muscle at any age, even while losing fat. The secret is strength training.

Strength training, also called resistance training, is exercise that makes your muscles work harder than they are accustomed to. As a result the muscle fibers become larger and stronger. To build your muscles, you can lift your own body weight against gravity (do sit-ups or push-ups), work against resistance (push an immobile object or push and pull rubber tubing), or lift weights (use free weights or exercise equipment designed for that purpose).

About 25 percent of your daily caloric need (metabolism) is driven by the amount of muscle tissue you have. Muscle is very metabolically active, while fat is not. The more muscle you have, the more calories you burn—even when you are at rest.

In fact, most of the age-related slowing of metabolism is due to the lack of physical activity and the loss of muscle tissue. This results in weight gain because when less energy is required for daily metabolic function, calories that were previously used by muscle tissue are stored as fat.

The effects of yo-yo dieting compound this problem. Every time you suddenly and drastically decrease your caloric intake without increasing your exercise, you lose as much, if not more, muscle as you do fat. Once you abandon the diet and resume eating the way you previously did, you will quickly regain fat—but not the muscle that you lost. As a result your metabolism will be even slower than it was; this can lead to more weight gain.

Benefits of Strength Training

Building your muscle tissue and increasing your strength has many benefits:

- Increases your ability to function in your daily life.
- Enables you to lift a heavy object.
- Enables you to lift a lighter object repeatedly.
- Boosts your metabolism.
- Improves your body composition by increasing your muscle mass relative to your total body weight.
- Helps you lose body fat.

- Minimizes the loss of lean body mass while eating to lose weight.
- Improves your physical appearance by creating a leaner, firmer body.
- Helps prevent age-related decreases in your muscle mass and increases in your body fat.
- Reduces your risk of injury by serving as shock absorbers during weight-bearing activities.
- Balances the strength of opposing muscle groups, which reduces the risk of overuse injuries.
- Decreases lower back pain by strengthening the core of the body.
- Increases your bone mineral density to prevent or treat osteoporosis.
- Improves your glucose metabolism.
- Lowers your blood pressure and cholesterol levels.
- Eases the pain from arthritis.
- Helps you appreciate the capacity of your body to meet the demands you place on it!

What You Need to Know

Many people don't realize the benefit of resistance training while they are trying to lose weight. With resistance exercise such as weight training, you will burn calories during *and* after exercise. Here's why. When you do a resistance exercise until the muscle is fatigued, the muscle undergoes microscopic damage. In the 24-48 hours following the exercise, the body repairs the damage and makes the muscle fiber larger and stronger to handle the increased work. The entire process burns calories. Furthermore, you burn calories each time you exercise to maintain your muscle tissue. Most importantly, the muscle you build will continue to burn calories even when it is just sitting still—so ultimately, you increase your metabolism through resistance training.

There will be remarkable changes going on in your muscles and you will notice your strength improve fairly quickly. However, it generally takes six to 24 weeks to notice significant changes in your appearance. Keep in mind that while the changes may or may not be evident on the scale, as your ratio of muscle to fat increases, you'll burn more calories, lose body fat, feel more comfortable in your clothes, and most importantly, become stronger and healthier.

Even people who do strenuous physical activity will benefit from strength training. They need to do specific exercises to balance the opposing muscles, to build the muscles that are neglected in their usual activities, and to improve their efficiency and performance. For example, a person who digs trenches and presumably has very strong back muscles should also do abdominal exercises. Someone who hikes regularly would also need to build upper-body strength. A tennis player would do strength training to increase the power behind his or her stroke.

You don't need to be concerned about getting too bulky or muscle bound from strength training. Most people do not have the genetic capability or the time required for training to gain that much muscle. Women have a relative lack of the male hormone testosterone so it is very unlikely they will bulk up. In fact, as muscle mass increases and body fat decreases, you will look leaner and lose girth—even if your weight doesn't change.

Get FITT

There are really two ways to look at muscle fitness. Muscular strength is the ability of a muscle to exert maximal force for a brief period of time. This is how much weight a person is able to lift once, for example, lifting a heavy suitcase into an overhead bin. Muscular endurance is the ability of a muscle or group of muscles to perform many repetitions against resistance, for example lifting a small child into the air repeatedly while playing. Resistance training will help you build both muscular strength and endurance.

You can vary strength training exercises by how much weight you lift or move, how much resistance you push or pull against, how long you hold a weight up against gravity, and how many times you repeat the exercise in a session. This last variable is usually measured in "reps" and "sets." Rep stands for repetition-lifting a weight or doing an exercise once. A set is a certain number of repetitions. For example, if you were to lift a hand weight 10 times, then rest and repeat, you did two sets of 10 reps.

Frequency: It will take a minimum of twice a week to see results. It is very important that you rest a muscle group for a minimum of 48 hours between weight training sessions to allow the muscles to repair.

Intensity: Do two to three sets of 8-20 repetitions per exercise. If you can't do a least eight repetitions, reduce the weight or resistance. If you can do more than 20 reps, increase the weight or resistance.

Time: The American College of Sports Medicine recommends 20-30 minutes of resistance training twice a week.

Type: You can increase your strength and muscle mass by lifting your own body weight (such as push-ups or sit-ups), using free weights, or exercise equipment for this purpose.

Simple Strength Training

Be certain to consult with your physician prior to beginning an exercise program. Consider seeking the advice of an exercise professional for a specific exercise prescription and instruction. Follow proper technique and form to decrease the chance of injuries and maximize your results.

There are many ways to build your strength. This simple routine can be done at home, in a hotel room, or even in your office, without any equipment. It utilizes your body weight against the resistance of gravity to help you build muscle. You will focus on your large core muscles so you will get the biggest bang for your buck.

It is important to prepare your muscles for strength training by performing a brief cardiorespiratory warm-up such as walking or cycling first. Start with as many repetitions as you can do comfortably. Even if you are only able to do one, if you practice repeatedly, your body will get stronger in order to meet the demands you are placing on it. As your fitness increases, repeat or hold each exercise 10 to 20 times or hold for 15 to 30 seconds per set. Start with one set then add one or two additional sets as you get stronger.

Do each exercise as slowly as possible and focus your attention on the muscles you are using. Exhale slowly during the part of the exercise that requires the most effort—for example, while doing leg lifts, exhale as you raise your leg and inhale as you lower it.

Squats

Muscles: Buttocks and legs

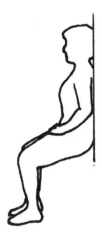

Stand with your back against a wall and your feet one thigh-length away from the wall. Bend your knees and lower yourself as if you were going to sit down. Press into the wall with your entire back while squeezing your buttocks and leg muscles. Eventually you will be able to get your thighs parallel to the ground. Hold as long as you can, for instance 15 to 30 seconds per set.

Modifications: Use an exercise ball between your back and the wall for additional support (it is easier to roll the ball down the wall to get into your "sit").

Push-ups

Muscles: Chest, shoulders, arms, and upper back

At the wall: Place your hands flat on a wall with your feet far enough away that you can push yourself away from the wall. Bend your elbows and slowly bring your body closer to the wall again. Repeat 10 to 20 times per set.

On your knees: While on all fours with your knees directly under your hips and your hands shoulder width apart, bend your elbows and lower your upper body toward the floor then press yourself back up. As you become stronger, move your knees further behind your hips. Repeat 10 to 20 times per set.

On your toes: Lie on your stomach with your hands positioned under your shoulders. Push your entire body off the ground while you are on your toes. Try to maintain a plank position as you slowly raise and lower your body toward the ground. Repeat up to 20 times per set.

Superman

Muscles: Lower back

Lie face down on the floor with your arms straight out in front of you. Lift your right arm and your left leg and hold for 15 to 30 seconds per set. Switch sides. As you get stronger, lift both legs and arms at the same time.

Modification: Position yourself comfortably on your hands and knees with your back level. Start by stretching your right arm out in front of you. If possible, straighten your left leg out at the same time. Hold for 15 to 30 seconds per set. Switch sides.

Leg Lifts

Muscles: Outer and inner thighs and buttocks

Lie on one side on the floor. Bend your bottom leg 45 degrees. Rest your head on your arm. Lift your top leg about halfway as you tighten your muscles in your buttocks and leg. Lift and lower your leg slowly 10 to 20 times per set. Roll to the other side and repeat.

Bridge

Muscles: Buttocks, thighs, lower back, and abdominals

Lie on your back on the floor. Bend your knees and place your feet hip distance apart. Tighten your buttocks and raise your hips off the floor then slowly lower down. Repeat 10 to 20 times per set. Alternatively, hold for 10 to 20 seconds per set.

Sit-ups

Muscles: Abdominals

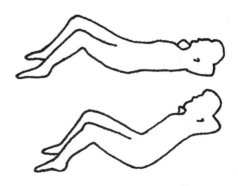

Lie on your back on the floor. Bend your knees and place your feet hip distance apart. Place your hands behind your head or cross your arms across your chest. Keep your neck in neutral position (don't flex your neck) and relax your arms and legs. Tighten the abdominal muscles to lift your upper body slowly then slowly lower down. Repeat 10 to 20 times per set.

Keep It Interesting

- Do resistance exercises at home with weights, elastic bands, rubber tubing, cans of food, or milk jugs partially filled with sand or water.

- A large exercise ball is one of the most versatile and affordable pieces of exercise equipment you can own. They are excellent for strength training (especially core strength), flexibility, balance, and coordination.

- Consider purchasing other home exercise equipment such as a weight bench or home gym if you enjoy the convenience and privacy of working out at home.

- Exercise in the water. Aquatic exercise enhances your cardiorespiratory fitness while the resistance of the water increases your muscular strength and endurance. Water also provides buoyancy and support for your body so there is less stress and strain on your joints and muscles.

- Hire a qualified and experienced personal trainer. Their expertise can help you set up a safe and efficient exercise program and help keep you motivated so you will reach your fitness goals.

- Join a gym. Choose a place that is convenient and feels comfortable. Most gyms will give you a free pass for a short period of time so you can make sure that it feels right to you.

- Check your community center for weight training, water aerobics, and other classes to help you build your strength.

- Consider signing up for a Boot Camp—an intensive regular group exercise program designed to rapidly improve your fitness.

- Try yoga. Yoga not only increases your flexibility and calms your mind, it builds a great deal of muscular strength and endurance with regular practice.

- As with other fitness activities, enlisting a friend to exercise with you will increase your motivation, accountability, and fun.

As you gain muscle tissue, you will find it easier to lose weight and maintain a healthier weight. For a limited investment in time, strength training will pay big rewards by increasing your metabolism and improving your muscular strength and endurance so you can function more fully in your life.

Nutrition: Essentials of Protein

Eating enough protein is vital for optimal health. Protein is found in every cell in your body and plays a role in basic bodily functions from walking to digesting food.

The Role of Protein in Your Health

One of the primary roles of protein is to build, repair, and maintain healthy muscles, organs, skin, and hair. Proteins are also critically involved in enzyme and hormone production, blood clotting, transportation of oxygen, maintenance of water balance, regulation of acid-base balance, and immune function. Protein can be broken down to provide the body with four calories of energy per gram if necessary.

Protein is made up of building blocks called amino acids. Just as the letters of the alphabet are arranged in different ways to make words, the 20 amino acids are arranged in different ways to build proteins with specific forms and functions.

Amino acids are classified as essential and non-essential. They are all important, but you must eat the nine essential amino acids in order for your body to make the protein it needs. On the other hand, your body can manufacture the 11 non-essential amino acids with the nitrogen it gets from other amino acids.

Protein is found readily in the food supply. Protein sources are categorized as complete or incomplete. A complete protein contains all of the essential acids, while an incomplete protein is missing one or more essential amino acid.

Animal sources of protein such as meat, poultry, fish, eggs, and dairy products are considered complete. The only non-animal complete protein source is soybeans. All other grains, beans, lentils, nuts, and seeds are incomplete protein sources.

Complementary proteins are two incomplete protein foods that compensate for the other's deficiencies in essential amino acid content. A classic example is rice and beans. By eating two complementary protein sources in the course of a day, all nine essential amino acids are available to make the necessary proteins.

Protein food sources also contain other important nutrients. For example, dairy products are a significant source of calcium. Beef is an excellent source of iron. Dairy and meat provide zinc and vitamins B6 and B12.

How Much Protein Do You Need?

Based on recommendations from various authorities, protein intake should fall in the range of 10 percent to 35 percent of total calories per day. On average, healthy adults should consume 0.75 grams of protein for every kilogram of their body weight (1 kilogram = 2.2 pounds). For example, a healthy 130 lb. woman needs approximately 47 grams of protein a day—a healthy 175 lb. man approximately 64 grams of protein a day.

A 130 lb. woman could easily consume 47 grams of protein by drinking an 8 ounce glass of milk in the morning, eating a chicken sandwich (3 ounce portion of chicken) for lunch, having 1 ounce of nuts as a snack, and eating 1/2 cup of legumes at dinner time. For a 175 lb. man, add 3 ounces of beef or fish to dinner and his requirement for protein will be met. Of course, these examples don't include grains, vegetables, or

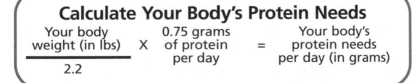

Calculate Your Body's Protein Needs

$$\frac{\text{Your body weight (in lbs)}}{2.2} \times \begin{array}{c} 0.75 \text{ grams} \\ \text{of protein} \\ \text{per day} \end{array} = \begin{array}{c} \text{Your body's} \\ \text{protein needs} \\ \text{per day (in grams)} \end{array}$$

additional dairy products, which would further increase the protein intake. The point is, your daily protein needs can be met easily without consuming a large amount of food.

A person that is growing, recovering from an illness, or doing athletic training will require more protein to build new tissues. These protein needs can generally be met through increased dietary intake; protein and amino acid supplements usually aren't needed.

Protein at a Glance

Source	Type	Amount of Protein per Serving	Serving Size
Dairy	Milk	8 grams	1 cup (8 oz.)
	Soft cheese (cottage or ricotta)	14 grams	1/2 cup (4 oz.)
	Hard cheese	5-7 grams	1 1/2 -2 oz.
	Yogurt	6-8 grams	8 oz.
	Ice cream	3-5 grams	1/2 cup
Eggs	Egg	6 grams	1
	Egg white	3.5 grams	1
	Egg substitute	5-6 grams	1/4 cup
Legumes	Beans or lentils	6-8 grams	1/2 cup
Meat, Poultry, or Seafood	Cooked lean meat, poultry or fish	6-9 grams per ounce	2-3 oz.
Nuts	Assorted nuts	6 grams	1 oz., 1/3 cup
	Peanut butter	8 grams	2 tablespoons
Soy	Soy, cooked	14 grams	1/2 cup
	Tofu	10 grams	1/2 cup

Getting the Most from Protein

Use the principles of balance, variety, and moderation as your guide to choosing your optimal sources of protein.

Balance: When you meet your hunger needs with a diet too heavy on protein (or any other nutrient), you are less likely to eat enough of the other important nutrients, which can lead to deficiencies in the long run. Besides, a lopsided diet becomes boring very quickly.

Variety: There are many ways to eat enough protein. The added bonus is that by increasing your variety, you will get other needed nutrients. For example, red meats are high in iron, legumes are high in fiber, and nuts are high in beneficial monounsaturated fats.

Moderation: As with any nutrient, if you take in more protein than your body needs, it will be used for energy or stored as fat. Additionally, excessive protein intake from animal sources can increase the risk of heart disease and cancer due to excessive intake of saturated fat.

To limit your saturated fat intake from your protein sources, consider the following suggestions:

- Select low-fat or fat-free dairy products such as skim or 1% milk, buttermilk, 2% or less fat cottage cheese, low-fat yogurt, and low-fat cheeses.
- Substitute whole eggs with egg whites or egg substitutes.
- Eat more fish.
- Use skinless chicken or turkey breast.
- Select the leanest available ground beef. Alternatively, after you brown ground beef, put it in a strainer and run very hot water over it to rinse some of the fat away.
- Select loin cuts of beef and pork.
- Try soy-based products.
- Opt for items that are grilled, broiled, baked, or poached instead of fried or served with heavy butter or cream-based sauces.
- For flavor, marinade meats, poultry, and fish in low-fat dressings, sprinkle on a fat-free seasoning mixture, or rub with a flavorful mixture of herbs and spices.

Health Notes: The Vegetarian Choice

Vegetarians do not eat meat, fish, poultry, or derivatives of these items, including animal fats such as lard, fish oils, gelatin, or casein. Lacto-ovo-vegetarians consume dairy products and eggs, whereas Vegans do not eat or use *any* animal products. People choose vegetarian lifestyles for ethical, religious, or health reasons.

With education and planning, a vegetarian diet can meet all of the body's nutrient needs. The key to a healthy vegetarian diet, as with any eating style, is to eat a wide variety of foods—including fruits, vegetables, leafy greens, whole grains, nuts, seeds, and legumes. Learning about complementary proteins and alternative sources of nutrients commonly found in animal protein will help you eat an adequate amount of essential and non-essential amino acids, micronutrients, and calories to meet your body's needs.

Even if you are not interested in a total vegetarian lifestyle, there are many advantages to going meatless sometimes. It is a healthful move because it has been shown to reduce the risk of heart disease, stroke, obesity, some forms of cancer, and adult-onset diabetes. Going meatless can be as easy as choosing pasta with tomato sauce, meatless chili, or a baked potato with the (low-fat) works. You can be more adventurous and incorporate exotic grains, new varieties of rice and vegetables, and tofu. Striking the right balance is dependent on your taste preferences and lifestyle. Try this approach:

Be Aware

- When do I eat meat most? When do I *enjoy* it the most—breakfast, dinner, weekends, while dining out?
- *When* would it be *easiest* for me to forgo meat?
- Which meats do I enjoy the most? Which could I live without or eat only on occasion?

Be Different

- Designate certain meals as meatless meals.

- Designate a certain number of days or specific days of the week as meatless. You may want to start with one or two days and gradually increase as you learn to enjoy other foods.

- Experiment with different meatless foods and recipes; try vegetarian recipes, tofu products, and meat substitutes.

- When visiting a restaurant, try a vegetarian item or ask for vegetarian substitutions. Ask the restaurant staff about the ingredients; some items appear to be vegetarian but may contain animal products such as lard.

Be Prepared

- Keep fast-cooking grain products on hand like pasta, couscous, quinoa, and white or brown rice. You can easily add sauces and vegetables for a quick meal.

- Stock up. Keep an assortment of canned beans such as pinto, kidney or garbanzo on hand. Enjoy bean burros or tostadas, and bean soups or salads.

- Dried beans are easy to cook—just throw them in the crockpot with plenty of water and seasonings and they are ready when you get home.

- Stock your freezer and pantry with vegetarian entrees and stir fry mixes.

- Make meals like vegetarian lasagna and chili ahead of time and freeze for later use.

Protein is a critical macronutrient involved in numerous bodily functions. It is easy to meet your daily protein needs when you consider balance, variety, and moderation in your food choices.

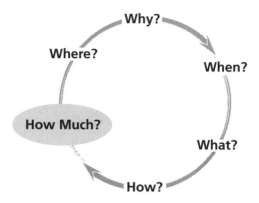

CHAPTER 7

Decision Point: How Much Do I Need?

Deciding how much food you need to eat is very important for lifelong weight management and health. Your awareness and the Hunger and Fullness Scale are the most useful tools for helping you master this Decision Point.

As with all of the other Decision Points in this system, the first and most important step is to fine-tune your awareness. As you learned in Chapter 4, to satisfy hunger but not overeat you need to make sure you are aware of how you feel physically when you are finished eating. Are you comfortable and content? Can you feel the food in your stomach? Does your stomach feel distended or full? Do you have any discomfort? Do you feel energetic or do you feel sleepy and sluggish? Based on your answers to these questions, you can determine your number on the Hunger and Fullness Scale *after* eating.

4 or Lower: When you are a 4 or lower, you are still a little hungry. Remind yourself that you may feel more full in a short while so plan to check back in with yourself again. If you are still at a 4 later, you could choose to eat a little more or wait awhile, then eat again. Notice that eating to a 4 is a great strategy if you are planning to have some dessert or if you will be eating again in a short while.

5 or 6: When you are a 5 or a 6, you will notice that you are not hungry anymore and you feel comfortable. You don't feel the food in your body; you could eat more but you don't need (or want) to. You will probably feel light and energetic. You may also notice that while you are eating, the flavor of the food goes from fabulous to just OK as you become less hungry. It becomes harder to give food and eating your full attention.

If you are a 5 or a 6, move away from the food—or move the food away from you to signal that you are finished. Pay close attention to this comfortable, contented, or even happy feeling and try to remember it for next time.

7 or Higher: At a 7 or above, you may think, "I ate too much!" You will feel uncomfortable and maybe even regretful. You might feel sleepy and sluggish. It is likely that it didn't even taste good by the end. In fact, you may have even stopped being *aware* that you were eating long before you actually stopped eating.

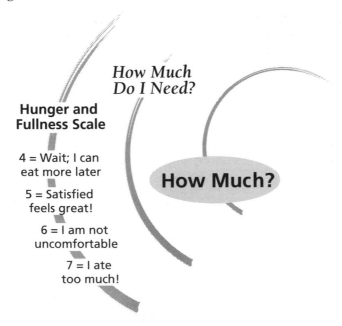

**Hunger and
Fullness Scale**

*How Much
Do I Need?*

4 = Wait; I can
eat more later

5 = Satisfied
feels great!

6 = I am not
uncomfortable

7 = I ate
too much!

How Much?

I Ate Too Much!

Think for a moment about what it means to be satisfied. Satisfied means that you simply don't need anything else—so you are left feeling contented, fulfilled, pleased, or even happy. How wonderful it is to feel satisfied when you are finished eating.

But it can be challenging too. People continue to eat past the point of satisfaction for many reasons: a result of habits and learned behaviors, a consequence of past dieting, and often, not paying attention while eating. The bottom line is that if you eat more than you need, you will feel unnecessarily uncomfortable and your body will have no choice but to store the excess as fat.

The most important part of this process is to observe your thoughts, feelings, and behaviors *non-judgmentally*. In other words, you are not going through this process to punish yourself, but to see what you can learn from the experience to increase the chance that you will do it a little better next time.

Compare learning to stop eating when you are satisfied, to teaching children to ride a bike.

Will they learn if you get angry or criticize them for their mistakes? Will they want to give up if they are expected to do it perfectly right away? Will they want to try again if they feel ashamed about what they have done?

Or will they learn best if you observe what they do, encourage each positive step they make, and offer gentle suggestions on how they can improve? Will they want to keep trying because you focus on how much they are improving, not on what they do wrong? Will they feel encouraged when they notice that it gets a little easier each time?

And like riding a bike, at some point, this process becomes automatic and natural. Eventually it won't require much effort or thought. Occasionally something will throw you off balance but you have practiced and learned to make necessary adjustments and corrections—so you keep on riding.

Notice How I Feel

If you feel too full after eating, sit quietly for a few moments and become completely aware of all of the feelings you have. Notice any discomfort, feeling of regret, or lack of pleasure.

Don't punish yourself for these feelings—but remember them in detail. The next time you are tempted to overeat, try to recall how you felt when you were too full so you will be less likely to repeat the mistake.

Why Did It Happen—and
What Will I Do Differently Next Time?

Now, ask yourself why it happened. Why do you think you overate? What is your plan for doing it differently next time? To change this pattern of behavior, ask yourself why you did it and make a plan to do it differently next time.

- **I wasn't hungry when I started eating.** When you eat before you are hungry, just about any amount of food will make you feel full. Work on waiting until you are a 2 or a 3 to eat.

- **I was too hungry when I started eating.** When you wait too long to eat, you are more likely to eat too much, too quickly and overshoot your stomach's comfortable capacity. Pay more attention to your hunger cues and be prepared to eat when you get to a 2 or a 3.

- **It just happened.** When you don't decide ahead of time how you want to feel at the end of the meal, you are more likely to overeat. In other words, start eating with an intention such as, "I will eat only as much as I need to feel comfortable at a 5." You can always change your mind but don't let it just happen—do it with full awareness of the consequences.

- **I wasn't paying attention as I ate.** When you eat while you are doing something else, you are less likely to enjoy your food or notice when you have had enough. Instead, choose to savor each bite without other distractions. Review How Will I Eat?

- **I ate too fast.** When you eat quickly, your fullness signals may not catch up, so you don't recognize that you are too full until it is too late. Slow down when you eat and pause for at least two minutes in the middle of eating. Ask yourself where you are on the Hunger and Fullness Scale.

- **I had too much on my plate.** Studies have shown that the larger the serving size, the more people eat. Make it a point to serve yourself only as much as you think you will need. When a large portion has been served to you, visually divide it into a more appropriate serving—or better yet, have the excess wrapped to go.

- **I was eating food that I didn't enjoy.** If you choose food that isn't really what you want, you may feel dissatisfied. You may continue to eat, trying to satisfy yourself, not realizing that the food choice is the problem, not the amount. If you realize you are eating a food that you don't really enjoy, stop and choose something else.

- **It tasted good so I kept eating it.** When you are eating a delicious food, you may get caught up in the experience and forget how it feels when you overeat. Remind yourself that if you keep eating, the discomfort will eventually outweigh the enjoyment.

- **I wanted the food to taste as good as it did at first.** Your taste buds are the most sensitive when you are hungry and when you first starting eating—so that is when food tastes the best. You may be tempted to keep eating because you want to experience those first wonderful bites again. But it won't taste that wonderful until you are hungry again.

- **I was worried that I wouldn't get that food again.** You may convince yourself that this is the only time you will get to have a particular food, so you should eat all you can. However, it is rare that a food will *never* be available again. You can ask for the recipe, take some home, plan to return to the same restaurant, ask the cook if they will make it for you again sometime, or enjoy experimenting with similar foods in the future.

- **I've been feeling deprived of that food.** If you haven't allowed yourself to have a certain food then you may overeat it when you finally give in. Remind yourself that there are no good or bad foods and that you can eat anything when you really want it and you are hungry. In fact, you are less likely to feel out of control around a certain food when you know that you can have it again whenever you want it.

- **I ate too much out of rebellion.** If someone has said you can't or shouldn't eat something, you may eat it all to spite him or her. But you are the one who is in charge of your eating—so you can choose what and how much you will eat.

- **It was a special occasion.** You are likely to overeat if you only give yourself permission to eat enjoyable foods on special occasions. You don't need an excuse to have a wonderful meal—so why use a special occasion as a special excuse to overeat? Just ask yourself why you would want to feel uncomfortable if the occasion is so special.

- **I wanted to taste everything!** Having a lot of food to choose from can be challenging. If you know this is difficult for you, you may choose to avoid buffets and similar settings whenever possible. Better yet, turn it around. Decide that with so many choices, you will get to eat exactly what you want. You get to be extremely picky so don't bother with anything ordinary!

- **I saved the best for last.** If you save your favorite food for the end of your meal, you may eat it even if you are already full. Instead, have at least a bite or two when it will taste the best; then if you are too full to finish it, it will be easier to save the rest for later.

- **I associated the event with overeating.** Many people learn to associate certain events with overeating— Thanksgiving dinner, Super Bowl parties, dinner at Grandmother's house. Be aware of these triggers so you can create new habits that suit you better than eating on autopilot.

- **I was keeping up with someone else.** You may overeat when someone else is eating a lot of food or very fast. You might be afraid that you won't get your share or you might think that you are not eating that much compared to the other person. Remember that you are eating to meet your needs, no one else's!

- **I like to feel full after a meal.** Over time you may have grown used to the full feeling you got from overeating. If you are having difficulty letting that go, try drinking water when you eat and load up on high fiber, bulky fruits, vegetables, and salads to fill you up without adding a lot more calories than your body needs. Then practice focusing on all of the negative consequences of being too full. Eventually you may begin to view fullness as a very unpleasant state that you wish to avoid.

- **I was eating out of obligation.** You may sometimes feel that you are expected to eat, such as when someone else made or bought the food. Food pushers may urge you to eat more than you want for many reasons, for example, to make themselves feel good, to show you that they care about you, or so they won't have to eat alone. Oftentimes no one really expects you to eat—but you think they do. Feeling obligated may cause you to ignore your body's signals of satisfaction in order to please someone else—or you may use it as an excuse to overeat. Remember that the reason you eat is to meet your own needs—not someone else's.

- **I wanted to get my money's worth.** When you have paid for something you may choose to eat more than you need so you won't feel that you have wasted your money. You might also be tempted to buy (and then eat) more than you need because it is a better value. However, the truth is, whenever you eat more than your body needs, your money has been wasted anyway.

- **I hate to let food go to waste.** This may come from your childhood: "Eat all your dinner; there are starving children in (fill in the blank)." Eating all of your food does not help children anywhere. If you are concerned about wasting food, take smaller portions, share meals, and save leftovers for another meal. Would you rather the food go to waste or waist?

- **I wanted to earn my dessert.** You are an adult now so you don't have to clean your plate if you want dessert. Instead, remember that other familiar phrase, Save room for dessert!

- **I kept eating to avoid or postpone doing something else.** Sometimes eating is a lot more fun than whatever else you think you should be doing. To combat this problem, make sure that you have something to look forward to (or at least that you don't dread doing) when you are finished eating.

- **I might be overeating to suppress other feelings.** This is the most challenging reason that people continue to eat past satisfaction. It may also be the most important. If you are eating instead of feeling your feelings or coping with your emotions, then you are not able to meet your true needs. The first step is to become aware of what is happening then make a decision to work on it, one step at a time. Surround yourself with supportive people and be gentle on yourself.

So, once you are aware that you have overeaten, first try to understand why it happened. Then create a plan for doing it differently. Paula shared this story:

> I had really cut down on my overeating. It didn't even feel good to be really full anymore. But I was still struggling with Sunday dinners at my grandmother's. The whole family had always joked about going off our diets once a week because she is such a wonderful cook. As soon as we get there, we start talking and nibbling on the cheese and crackers or other snacks that she puts out. She serves this amazing dinner but there is always way more food

than one family should eat. Somehow she manages to goad us into "finishing it all off so it won't go to waste."

I noticed that I always felt miserable by the time we left. When I observed her bribing my kids with dessert for finishing the huge plate of food she gave them, I suddenly realized that I am an adult now and I am in charge of what and how much I will eat. I decided to be more aware of what I was eating instead of falling into my old habits. I also decided to talk to my grandmother but I was worried about hurting her feelings so I practiced what I was going to say ahead of time—and I made sure it was sincere. Finally, last week I said, "Grandma, this was another of your great meals! I couldn't be more satisfied but I hope you will teach me how to make this sometime." Do you know that she packed me up a "to go" container to take to work the next day. Next time I am going to gently ask her to let my kids fill their own plates and remind them to save room for her wonderful desserts.

When Do I Want to Eat Again?

When you have overeaten, first observe how long it takes for you to get hungry again. When you overeat your body will not need food as soon as it does when you eat a smaller amount. Therefore, you may not be hungry for your usual snack or even your next meal. Don't eat the next meal just because it is time. Ramona is working on freeing herself from that trap:

My husband has always been an instinctive eater. I used to get so mad at him because I would work all afternoon preparing lasagna or something else, but sometimes he would just pick at it. He would say that he just wasn't that hungry because they had gone out for Mexican food for lunch. I used to try to get him to eat anyway because I was thinking, 'Hey! It's lasagna, and I made it, and you should want to eat it no matter what else you ate today!' But now I understand. In fact I realized that quite often, I wasn't really all that hungry either. It dawned on me that I had gotten in to the habit of tasting a lot while I was cooking. I am trying to break that habit, but now, if one of us isn't hungry, we just wrap it up so we can have it for lunch or dinner the next day when we will actually enjoy it.

What Am I Hungry For Then?

When you do get hungry again, ask yourself, "What do I want?" and "What do I need?" You might notice that you are hungry for something light—maybe fruit or a salad. Respect and honor what your body is telling you.

Putting It All Together

Here is the strategy for learning to recognize and stop at satisfaction.

Stopping when you are satisfied instead of too full is an important step for lifelong weight management. Feeling satisfied feels great and becomes easier and more natural with each positive experience.

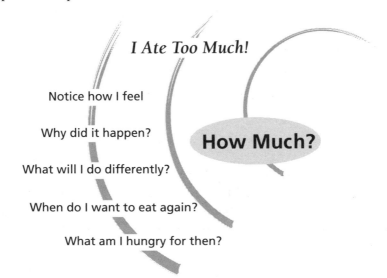

I Ate Too Much!

Notice how I feel

Why did it happen?

What will I do differently?

When do I want to eat again?

What am I hungry for then?

How Much?

Fitness: Taking Charge of Your Fitness

If you have been doing some form of regular activity up to this point, you have probably already begun to see some of the many benefits. Even if you just recently started, you may already feel better, both physically and mentally. To obtain the optimal benefit from your fitness program, it really pays to stay motivated and keep it challenging so that you gradually and continually improve your level of fitness.

Attitude Is Everything

In order to get past the common temptation to give up your fitness program when you lose motivation or don't see immediate results, first observe your own internal dialogue. Once you recognize the subtle negative self-talk, you will find it much easier to stay on track. Listen for messages like:

- *This is never going to work anyway; it's not worth it.*
- *I've been doing this for seven weeks now and I can hardly see the difference.*
- *It's not fair that I have to exercise to lose weight.*
- *I'll never be able to do this; it is too hard.*
- *I'll do it later when I have more time.*
- *I hate to exercise!*

Write down the messages you say to yourself. If they are negative, counter them in a positive way. Pretend that you are trying to convince a friend to do something to feel and look better *and* experience health improvements. After all, isn't that what you are really doing? Remember that attitude is everything. (Review Build a Positive Attitude About Exercise for more ways to counter your negative self-talk.) Practice giving yourself positive messages:

- *I'm building a healthier, leaner body, little by little.*

- *My clothes fit better and I have more stamina and energy than before.*
- *I feel a lot better after exercising.*
- *It seems a little easier each time I do it.*
- *A work-out is a great way to get rid of my stress.*
- *This feels great!*

Remember, your thoughts affect your feelings, and your feelings affect your behaviors. By repeating these positive thoughts frequently, you are more likely to think positively about exercise and develop the exercise habit.

Go for the Goal

Some of the benefits of exercise develop gradually so you may miss them if you're not looking. Make a point of identifying the gains that occur with each session by setting small goals for yourself and then record your progress in some measurable way on a graph. Some ideas:

- Number of days that you are consistently active.
- Number of times you took the stairs, walked to the mailbox, parked far away, etc.
- Number of activity sessions per week, or number of short sessions each day.
- Number of repetitions and sets of strength training.
- Time it takes to cover a specific distance.
- Minutes at a certain recorded speed on a treadmill or bike.
- Number of steps you take each day (recorded on a pedometer).
- Amount of time spent walking, dancing, swimming, biking—whatever.
- Distance (in blocks, laps, miles, etc.)
- Any other measurement of your frequency, intensity, time, and type of exercise.

You will be surprised at how much you can accomplish with a regular program. Stay motivated by setting specific, measurable goals. Write your goals down as a positive statement. Some examples:

- I will play actively with my children every day.
- I will walk my dog for 15 minutes before and after work.
- I will walk up the two flights of stairs to my office instead of using the elevator.
- I will walk four times a week to prepare for a 5K walk next fall.
- I will do twenty minutes of strength training three times a week.
- I will join a tennis league this week.
- I will sign up for yoga classes at the community center.
- I will ask a friend to commit to going for a hike with me once a week.

Reward Yourself

Through these fitness sections you have learned about all the ways that exercise benefits your health and well-being. However, it may take a little while for you to see all of these intrinsic rewards. In the meantime, it may help for you to set up an extrinsic reward system (in other words, an immediate tangible benefit for your efforts) in order to encourage yourself. Once you have set your activity goals, reward yourself for achieving those goals. Here are a few suggestions:

- Deposit a small sum of money for each session into a jar to spend on yourself.
- Treat yourself to a hot bath, foot massage, healthy snack, leisure time to read a favorite book or listen to music—or anything else that makes you feel good.
- Buy yourself an activity-related item like exercise clothing, athletic shoes, music to listen to while you work-out,

exercise equipment, gym membership, or personal training sessions.

Getting the Most From Your Activity

The FITT Principle is an important guide for maintaining and changing your physical activity levels. Remember FITT stands for; Frequency, how often you do the activity; Intensity, how much effort you use; Time,how long you do the activity; and Type, what activities you choose to do. All of these variables can be adjusted to help you obtain the optimal benefit from your fitness program.

An important question to ask when you are evaluating and planning your fitness program is, "How can I get the *most* out of my activities in the *least* amount of time?" The answer to this question lies in the *intensity* at which you exercise—in other words, the amount of effort you put into it. After Bridget learned about the importance of intensity, she told us that she realized the she had been fake exercising.

I was just going through the motions, not challenging myself at all. When I realized that I was probably wasting a lot of my time, I committed myself to putting in the effort that my body deserves. I am already starting to notice an improvement in my level of fitness and I feel great!

Make sure the intensity of your fitness program is optimal in order to keep your fitness program challenging and efficient. This will decrease the likelihood that you will quit due to boredom or lack of results.

There are many ways to measure the intensity of exercise. The easiest way is the talk test. You should be able to carry on a conversation while you exercise. If you are breathless, slow down. If you can sing, give your activity more effort.

Two other ways to measure your intensity include taking your heart rate reading and using the Perceived Exertion Scale.

Check Your Heart Rate

After at least five minutes of exercise, slow down briefly and check your pulse. You can find your pulse by gently resting two fingers on the side of your neck (next to your Adam's apple) or on the thumb side of your wrist. Count your pulse for one minute. It may be easier to count for six seconds and multiply by 10, or count for 15 seconds and multiply by four to get your 60-second pulse.

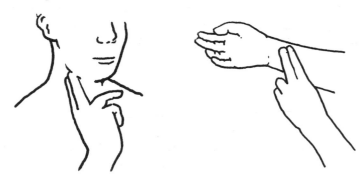

Target Heart Rate (THR)

For cardiovascular activities, you will achieve the optimal benefit by keeping your heart rate in the Target Heart Rate (THR) zone. This zone is between 65 and 90 percent of your Maximal Heart Rate (MHR). To find your Target Heart Rate (THR) zone use these equations:

Estimated Maximal Heart Rate (MHR) = 220 - Your Age
Low end of your THR zone = 65% of Maximal Heart Rate
= 0.65 x MHR
High end of your THR zone = 90% of Maximal Heart Rate
= 0.90 x MHR

For example, the Target Heart Rate zone for a 40 year old would be:

Maximal Heart Rate = 220 - 40 = 180
Low end of THR zone = 0.65 x 180 = 117
High end of THR zone = 0.90 x 180 = 162

When first starting a fitness program, you should exercise at 55 percent to 64 percent of your Maximal Heart Rate. As you become accustomed to exercising, you will feel comfortable when you exercise in your optimal Target Heart Rate zone. If your heart is beating slower than the low end of your target heart rate zone, then you will not get the optimal benefits from your exercise so you may wish to exert more effort. If your heart is beating faster than the high end of your target heart rate zone, then you are exercising too hard so you need to slow down.

The Perceived Exertion Scale

Since the equation 220 minus your age is just an estimate of exercise intensity, you can also use a subjective index, called the Perceived Exertion Scale (similar to the widely used Borg RPE Scale) to assess your level of effort, strain, or discomfort felt during exercise. (If you are on medication that alters your heart rate, such as a beta-blocker, use the Perceived Exertion Scale).

The Perceived Exertion Scale

Very Weak		Moderate		Strong		Very Strong			Maximal
1	2	3	4	5	6	7	8	9	10

Maximize your exercise intensity by keeping yourself within the Target Heart Rate zone of 65 percent to 90 percent of your maximal heart rate or a Perceived Exertion Level between 3 and 5 (moderate to strong). When assessing your level of Perceived Exertion, remember to take into account your health, your fitness level, degree of fatigue, and the environmental conditions. A Perceived Exertion Level of 1 to 2 is recommended when first starting a fitness program.

Keep It Interesting

One of the most common reasons for giving up an exercise program is boredom. If your activities are not enjoyable, interesting, challenging, fun, or rewarding in some way, you may lose interest. If you find yourself dreading your exercise instead of looking forward to it, consider making a few changes:

- Make sure your choice of activity fits your preferences and lifestyle.

- Make a small change to your regular routine; for instance, try a different time of day, two shorter sessions instead of one longer one, a new route, or even your same route backwards.

- Mix it up a bit by trying new activities once in awhile. If you usually walk, try a gentle hike; if you ride a stationary bike, ride outside; if you do ballet, try yoga; if you do aerobics, take a dance class.

- Vary your activities during the week like walking, swimming, stretching, and strength training. This will keep you from getting bored and gives you the benefit of a complete fitness program.

- Be efficient and productive. Tape your favorite show to watch while you exercise. Do floor exercises or stretches while you read your mail. Spend time with your children playing. Ask your partner or a friend to join you.

- Learn a new sport or practice a new skill.

- Have fun!

Your Top Priority—You!

By far the most common reason people don't exercise is a perceived lack of time. You must keep reminding yourself that regular exercise is more important than just about anything you can choose to do with your time. Besides, an active lifestyle will make you healthier and happier so you will be even more productive in other areas of your life.

The key is to schedule time for exercise and write it down in your planner, just as you would any other important appointment. If you can't make the exercise appointment at the scheduled time, you simply reschedule within a reasonable period of time just as you would reschedule any other appointment. Be as consistent and as flexible as possible so your fitness program will fit into your life.

You'll be surprised at how soon regular exercise will become a part of your routine, much like brushing your teeth. You'll actually miss it when you can't fit it in. Take charge of building a regular fitness program and look for ways to keep yourself motivated—the rewards are well worth it.

Nutrition: Essentials of Micronutrients and Nutrition Labels

You now have a better understanding of the macronutrients—carbohydrates, protein, and fat. It is time to turn your attention to micronutrients—vitamins, minerals, electrolytes, anti-oxidants, phytochemicals and other nutrients found in small amounts in your diet.

Vitamins and minerals perform hundreds of vital functions in the body and are essential for life. Although much is known about these nutrients, ongoing research is discovering new functions and other vital components in food.

Identifying all of the different micronutrients, understanding their various roles, and knowing which foods contain them can be overwhelming. In truth, you do not need to memorize all of this information to build optimal health. Instead, focus on the things that are most relevant to your life. Choose a variety of healthful, tasty foods and consider the addition of a multi-vitamin/mineral supplement daily. You will likely get all the nutrients you need to be healthy and feel great.

The following Vitamin and Mineral reference chart outlines various vitamins and minerals, their major roles, common food sources, and the recommended intake.

Vitamins and Minerals at a Glance

Vitamins	Significant Sources	Major Physiological Functions
Vitamin A (retinol, retinal, carotene)	Yellow/orange fruits & vegetables: carrots, sweet potatoes, cantaloupe; watermelon, dark green leafy vegetables, spinach, tomatoes, broccoli liver, milk, margarine	Promotes eye health, protection against night blindness helps keep skin healthy and helps body resist infection, building strong bones and teeth
Recommended Amts: Women, 11 yrs and up: 800 mcg; Men, 11 yrs and up: 1000 mcg		
Vitamin D	Exposure to sun, fortified milk, small amounts of butter, liver, egg yolk, salmon, sardines, fish-liver oils	Increases calcium and phosphorous absorption and utilization, helps bones and teeth harden
Recommended Amts: Adult >24 yrs: 5 mcg (200 IU) or appx. 15 mins in the sun		
Vitamin E	Vegetable oils, margarine, butter, eggs, whole grains, wheat germ, liver, leafy greens	Works as antioxidant preventing destruction of vitamins A, C, fatty acids and cell membranes
Recommended Amts: Women: 8 mg/day; Men: 10 mg/day		
Vitamin K	Leafy green vegetables, milk, soybean oil, egg yolks, intestinal bacteria synthesizes most of the vitamin K the body needs	Helps the clotting action of blood in wounds
Recommended Amts: 1 mcg/kg of body weight		
Vitamin C	All citrus fruits and juices, strawberries, mango, cantaloupe, papaya, Brussels sprouts, tomatoes, green/red peppers, cabbage, spinach, broccoli, kale and turnip greens, potatoes, mustard greens	Forms glue that holds body cells together, strengthens blood vessels, promotes iron absorption, speeds healing, boosts immune system
Recommended Amts: 60 mg/day		
Folate, Folic Acid	Legumes, oranges, strawberries, green leafy vegetables, asparagus, whole grains, sunflower seeds, liver	Promotes red blood cell formation greatly reduces birth defects of brain and spine, recent evidence shows reduces risk of heart disease
Recommended Amts: Women (not pregnant or lactating): 180 mcg; Men: 200 mcg		
Vitamin B12	Animal products: meat, fish, poultry, eggs, milk and milk products	Assists in maintenance of nerve tissue and normal blood cell formation
Recommended Amts: Adults: 2 mcg		

Vitamins	Significant Sources	Major Physiological Functions
Vitamin B6, pyridoxine	Poultry, fish, pork, unprocessed whole grains, legumes, potatoes, sweet potatoes, nuts, avocados, bananas, brewer's yeast	Necessary for metabolism of protein, needed to build certain amino acids and turn others into hormones, helps build red blood cells and maintain nerve tissue, metabolizes polyunsaturated fats
Recommended Amts: Women: 1.6 mg/day; Men: 2.0 mg/day		
Niacin (B3)	Meat, poultry, fish, liver, peanuts, legumes, whole grain or enriched cereals and breads	Helps the body produce energy from carbohydrate and fat; plays a role in maintaining healthy skin, nerves, & digestive system
Recommended Amts: 6.6 niacin equivalents per 1,000 kcal		
Riboflavin (B2)	Meat, liver, fish, milk, yogurt, cheese, eggs, dark green leafy vegetables, enriched breads and cereals,	Plays a role in healthy skin and eyes, is a part of enzymes that cells use to produce energy
Recommended Amts: Adults: 1.2 mg/day		
Thiamin (B1)	Legumes, whole grains, cereals, sunflower seeds, nuts, pork, liver, other meats	Is a key part of enzymes that are needed to turn carbohydrate into energy; promotes normal appetite and nerve function
Recommended Amts: Adults: 1.0 mg/day		
Calcium	Milk, yogurt, cheese, collard greens, fortified orange juice and other products, salmon and sardines with bones	Builds and maintains strong bones and teeth; helps muscles contract and relax normally
Recommended Amts: 19-50 yrs: 1000 mg; >51 yrs: 1200 mg (not pregnant or lactating)		
Iron	Meat (especially beef), seafood, legumes, dried fruits, fortified cereals	Builds red blood cells to maintain healthy blood and transport oxygen in body
Recommended Amts: Women: 15 mg/day; Men: 10-12 mg/day		

Vitamins	Significant Sources	Major Physiological Functions
Magnesium	Unprocessed foods; whole seeds such as nuts, legumes, and unmilled grains; green vegetables; bananas	Numerous biochemical and physiological processes require or are modulated by Magnesium. Critical to the transmission of impulses and electrical potentials of nerves and muscle membranes
Recommended Amts: Adults: 4.5 mg/day		
Potassium	Vegetables, milk, yogurt, meat, poultry, fish and fruits	Helps the body maintain normal blood pressure and cell functions
Recommended Amts: Adults: 1,600 to 2,000 mg/day		
Sodium	Table salt (1/4 tsp = 2400 mg), most prepared foods	Used by the body to control blood pressure and blood volume
Recommended Amts: <2400 mg/day		
Zinc	Meat, liver, eggs, seafood, cereals	No single enzyme function has been determined, however, a deficiency of zinc may cause loss of appetite, growth retardation, skin changes, and immunologic abnormalities
Recommended Amts: Women: 12 mg/day; Men: 15 mg/day		

Focus on Foods

Foods are the best source of nutrients because, unlike supplements, they provide nutrients in a natural balance that can be well absorbed. Since nutrients are found in varying amounts in different foods, it is important to focus on variety when planning your meals and snacks. If your choices are excessive in one macronutrient but lacking in another, you risk missing out on important nutrients. It is also important to eat a variety of foods within each category since no one food provides all of the essential micronutrients.

However, it is not necessary to know exactly how much of each nutrient a food contains, or even exactly what each nutrient does, as long as you are focusing on variety, balance, and moderation.

Taking Vitamins and Minerals

In today's busy lifestyle, it is sometimes difficult to make sure that you are getting all of the nutrients you need. Taking a daily multivitamin/mineral supplement can help fill in the gaps. Choose a brand or generic brand that has USP (United States Pharmacopoeia) on the label to ensure that it contains the amount of the ingredients listed and will dissolve properly. Look for a multivitamin with about 100 percent of the Daily Value for most nutrients, and take it with a meal for maximal absorption.

The Recommended Dietary Allowance (RDA) is set by the Food and Nutrition Board of the National Research Council. It is important to understand that the RDAs are set to meet the body's needs but are actually *more* than most people require.

When you exceed the RDA, most of the excess water-soluble vitamins are excreted in your urine. On the other hand, fat soluble vitamins (Vitamins A, D, E, K) when taken in excess, accumulate in the body and can reach toxic levels over a period of time or interfere with the function of other vitamins and minerals.

Understanding Antioxidants and Phytochemicals

Our bodies are assaulted constantly by free radicals, toxic by-products of oxidation, the process our bodies use to burn fuel with oxygen. We also accumulate free radicals from our environment (i.e. tobacco smoke, pollution and ultraviolet light). These free radicals, in excess, can cause fatigue, disease, and aging.

So what's a body to do? You may have heard about antioxidants which have been shown to improve health and boost the immune system. Plants produce antioxidants to protect themselves from the free radicals formed during photosynthesis. Some studies have shown that *our* free radicals can be neutralized by eating plant foods rich in these antioxidants. The vitamins C, E, and beta-carotene and minerals such as zinc, selenium, copper, and magnesium are necessary for some of the reactions to occur. However, taking antioxidants in a supplement form (often sold in doses above the RDA) to prevent certain diseases is not proving to be as promising as scientists had hoped. The health-protective benefit seems to come by eating antioxidant-rich foods.

In addition, credible scientific research has shown that small chemical compounds called phytochemicals also with powerful antioxidant properties are found naturally in a variety of flavorful plants. Because antioxidants protect the surfaces of the plant from damage, they are found in the skin and outer surfaces of grains, beans, fruits, and vegetables. Presently, over 25,000 phytochemicals have been identified, among them, Carotenoids, Lycopene, Sulforaphane, Flavenoids, and Isoflavones. There is strong evidence to show that phytochemicals reduce the risk of cataracts, cancer, and heart disease.

Power Foods

Some plant foods are packed with nutrients and healthful phytochemicals. Here are some examples of these Power Foods. By consuming some of these every day, you may increase your nutrition considerably.

Vegetables	Fruits	Grains/Nuts	Herbs
Broccoli	Blueberries	Almonds	Garlic
Carrots	Grapes	Brown rice	Ginger
Kale	Guava, Mango	Legumes (beans, lentils)	Green tea
Pumpkins	Melon	Soy, Tofu	Parsley
Spinach	Strawberries	Walnuts	Rosemary
Sweet Potatoes	Tomatoes	Whole Wheat	Thyme

Maximize the Nutrients in Your Food

- Go for color. The more deeply colored the flesh of fruits and vegetables, the more phytochemicals they are likely to have.

- Fresh is best. Just storing fruits and vegetables for a prolonged time will cause them to lose some of their nutrients. If you cannot buy and eat your produce at the freshest possible stages, fresh frozen is the next best thing.

- Eat the skins and peels whenever possible. Remember to wash them thoroughly before cooking or eating.

- Cook vegetables just to the tender-crisp stage so they look and taste their best and retain more nutrients. Use a minimum amount of water so you don't lose the vitamins when they are drained. Better yet, steam them using a steamer or colander in a covered pot with a small amount of boiling water. Stir-frying is another quick and easy method to cook vegetables with relatively little fat, and preserving the crisp texture, bright color, and maximum nutrients of the vegetables.

- Organic foods are more readily available than ever. Whether they are more nutritious is difficult to study since there are so many variables that can affect the nutrient content. In any case, it is always best to thoroughly wash all fruits and vegetables prior to consumption.

- If you drink, red wine in moderation may provide some benefits. It is possible that these same benefits can be found in grape juice.

Choosing a variety of foods packed with nutrition will provide your body with what it needs to look and feel great.

Understanding the Food Label

Now you have the essentials of macronutrients (carbohydrates, fats, and protein) and micronutrients. The food label is a helpful tool for making informed decisions about these nutrients when buying and preparing food. Reading nutrition labels is a great way to learn more about the nutrient content of foods but they should *not* be misused to deprive you of certain foods, restrict you from certain ingredients like fat or carbohydrates, or force you to ignore your body's signals about what it wants and needs. Labels simply provide information so you can make an educated choice.

Nutrition Claims

You will often find nutrition claims listed on the front of a package describing various nutritional qualities. These descriptors can be helpful if you know what they mean.

Basic Terminology

Free:

- Calorie-free: 5 calories or less per serving.
- Fat-free: less than 0.5 grams of fat (or 0.5 grams of saturated fat) per serving.
- Cholesterol-free: less than 2 mg of cholesterol per serving.
- Sugar-free: less than 0.5 grams of sugar per serving.

Low:

- Low Calorie: 40 calories or less per serving.
- Low Fat: 3 grams or less of fat (or 1 gram of saturated fat) per serving.
- Low Cholesterol: 20 mg or less of cholesterol per serving.
- Low Sodium: 140 mg or less of sodium per serving.
- Low Carb: There are currently no guidelines for the use of this term.

Reduced, Less, Fewer — As in Reduced Calories or Less Fat: A product contains at least 25 percent less (calories, sugar, or fat) than a similar product.

Light: One third fewer calories, half the fat, or half the sodium of a similar food. Caution: light can also describe texture and color of the product.

Lean: A serving of meat, poultry, or seafood containing less than 10 grams of fat, 4.5 grams of saturated fat and 95 grams of cholesterol.

Extra Lean: Less than 5 grams of fat, 2 grams of saturated fat, and 95 mg of cholesterol.

Health Claims

Solid: These claims are based on reliable evidence and approved by the FDA. A specific disease will be stated such as "A diet low in total fat may reduce the risk of heart disease."

Preliminary: These are based on incomplete or unreliable evidence and will include a disclaimer like "The FDA has determined evidence as inconclusive."

Structure/Function: These unreliable claims do not require any evidence. Look for words like "maintains" (as in maintains bone health) and "supports" (as in supports the immune system). These are found on food and supplements and require no approval by the FDA.

Nutrition Facts

There are various items located under the title Nutrition Facts. Here is a brief overview with helpful tips for interpretation.

Serving Size: Check the listed serving size; one package may actually be four servings. The portions listed are not necessarily *recommended* amounts; they are approximations of what most people eat. If it is inconvenient to measure your serving, use the Serving Per Container to estimate serving (for example, one fourth of the container). Don't forget, Hunger and Fullness levels should be driving how much you eat, not just the label.

The nutrient information and Percent Daily Values listed on the food label are based on one serving. If the serving size is one cup and you consume two cups, multiply all numbers by two.

Calories: Calories (i.e. total) and calories from fat are listed under the Amount Per Serving information. (Total calories includes calories from fat.) Calories give us energy; but remember, if you consume more than needed, they are stored as fat. Looking at calories may help you determine if certain food items are pushing you over the edge in your quest for energy balance.

Nutrition Facts

Serving Size 1 cup (228g)
Servings Per Container 2

Amount Per Serving

Calories 260   Calories from Fat 120

	% Daily Value*
Total Fat 13g	**20%**
Saturated Fat 5g	**25%**
Cholesterol 30mg	**10%**
Sodium 660mg	**28%**
Total Carbohydrate 31g	**10%**
Dietary Fiber 0g	**0%**
Sugars 5g	
Protein 5g	

Vitamin A 4%	Vitamin C 2%
Calcium 15%	Iron 4%

*Percent Daily Values are based on a 2,000 calorie diet. Your daily values may be higher or lower depending on your calorie needs.

	Calories	2,000	2,500
Total Fat	Less than	65g	80g
Saturated Fat	Less than	20g	25g
Cholesterol	Less than	300mg	300mg
Sodium	Less than	2,400mg	2,400mg
Total Carbohydrate		300g	375g
Dietary Fiber		25g	30g

Calories per gram:
Fat 9 • Carbohydrate 4 • Protein 4

Percent Daily Value (%DV): Keeping track of your daily intake can be time consuming, tedious and, in most cases, unnecessary. However, knowing how much you are getting of a certain nutrient can be beneficial. Percent Daily Values were designed to help consumers quickly see how much of their daily needs are being met through the selected food item. In an ideal situation (where you had a food label for everything you ate), adding up each nutrients' %DV would indicate how well you were meeting your nutrient needs. Being close to 100% DV for each item would indicate a well-balanced daily intake.

Located on the right side of the label, %DVs are reference numbers based on a person who consumes 2,000 calories a day.

This may be more or less than what *your* body needs. Although not exactly individualized, %DV can be used to evaluate the food in hand. For nutrients we want to eat more of, like fiber and calcium, you want to see higher %DVs. For those nutrients we want to eat less of, like fat, cholesterol, and sodium, look for lower %DVs.

Fat: Recall that the recommendation for fat is an intake of 30 percent or less of calories from fat and no more than 10 percent of calories from saturated fat. On the label, total fat and saturated fat are listed in grams (g) and as a %DV. The %DV is based on 65 g of total fat (30 percent of a 2,000 calorie diet) and 20 g of saturated fat (10 percent of a 2,000 calorie diet). That doesn't mean you shouldn't eat a food that is higher than 30 percent for the DV; it simply means that you will want to balance it by selecting other lower fat foods. For example, you may select cheese (a higher fat food) but accompany it with wheat crackers or fruit (lower fat foods).

Cholesterol: Due to the prevalence of heart disease, cholesterol is listed on the label. It is listed in milligrams (mg) and as a %DV. The %DV is based on 300 mg of cholesterol. If your doctor has provided stricter guidelines due to heart health, you may find it easier to track your cholesterol intake in milligrams.

Sodium: Sodium is a mineral that is used by the body to control blood pressure and blood volume. Most nutrition experts recommend a daily maximum of less than 2,400 milligrams of sodium. The amount of sodium in a serving of food is listed in milligrams (mg) and as % Daily Value.

Carbohydrates: These are listed as Total (in grams and % DV), Dietary Fiber (in grams and % DV based on 25 grams per day), and Sugars (in grams only). If you subtract Dietary Fiber and Sugars from the Total grams, the remaining number is the grams of starch. A food with five grams or more of fiber is considered high fiber.

Protein: Listed in grams per serving. Compare this with the personal daily protein needs that you calculated previously.

Vitamins: The food label also lists % DV for Vitamin A, Vitamin C, Calcium, and Iron. Others may be listed; only these four are required. This information will help you target nutrient rich foods, but the best way to ensure that you get all of the vitamins and minerals you need is by eating a wide variety. See Micronutrients for more details.

Ingredient List

Ingredient lists tell you what was used to prepare the food. They are listed in order from the most to the least based on weight. This list is helpful if you have allergies, prefer not to eat certain things, or want information about additives and preservatives. Looking for hydrogenated or partially hydrogenated oils will indicate the presence of trans fat.

Preparation Instructions

Notice the differences between "as packaged" and "as prepared." As packaged gives the nutrition information for what is in the container. As prepared includes all ingredients when prepared according to the package directions. Comparing this information can help you decide if preparation substitutions are beneficial.

For convenience, many packages already include lower fat version preparation instructions. You can also make your own substitutions to boost the nutrient content or lower the calorie content. Some examples: Add extra vegetables (fresh or frozen) to just about any side dish or entree. Use skim milk in place of whole milk or cream. Skip or reduce the butter, margarine, or oil in stuffing, pasta, potato, and rice products. For example, the directions may include 2% milk and butter but to lower the saturated fat content, you could use skim milk and half the amount of butter. Note: Substitutions like this are usually more successful and less noticeable with packaged rice, pastas, soups, and casseroles than with baked goods. You can substitute egg whites or egg substitute for whole eggs and part of the oil in baked goods with applesauce or pureed prunes (found in baby food jars).

Practical Strategies

- Nutrition labels are also available for fresh meats, seafood, and produce—just ask your grocer.

- Don't forget to check the label on your vitamin/mineral supplements, but remember, more of a good thing is not necessarily better.

- Many fast food and chain restaurants have nutrition information available. This might help to make a decision between two equally appealing entrees.

- Many foods that claim "reduced fat" or "low carb" have substituted other ingredients and may have as many calories as the original. If you are going to pay attention to the front of the label, you have to look at the back too!

- Although reduced, light, or low products can help you reach your health goals, if it doesn't taste good to you, you won't feel satisfied when you eat it. In that case, it is better to stick with the original version and eat it less often or in smaller amounts. Remember, no food is forbidden.

Use the Nutrition Facts to educate yourself about the nutrient content of food, *not* to label food as "good' or "bad." Labels are an important way to be informed and ultimately improve your health and well-being.

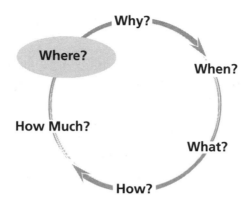

CHAPTER 8

Decision Point: Where Does My Energy Go?

As you free yourself from thinking about food as "good" or "bad," you can also free yourself from thinking about where you use energy as just exercise.

Where your energy goes is much more than just burning calories. In this diet-crazed culture, what should be the natural process of consuming fuel in order to supply the necessary energy to survive and thrive has instead become a national pastime—or more accurately, an obsession. Remember that the real reason that you eat is to fuel your life and give you the energy to do whatever you need and want to do.

So what do *you* want to do? Where do you want to invest *your* energy?

Optimal Health

Am I Hungry? has given you the tools to listen to your hunger cues, enjoy food again, and develop a healthier, active lifestyle without following a rigid diet or exercise regimen. But

the most powerful result of freeing yourself from your Over Eating and Restrictive Eating Cycles is that you will have more energy to focus on what it really takes to make you a healthy person.

Throughout this book, we referred to optimal health. Optimal health is a state of physical, emotional, intellectual, and spiritual wellness.

Optimal health does not mean perfect health. Optimal health is the best health you can have, given your individual situation. For example, a person with cancer does not have perfect health but it is possible for them to have optimal health through appropriate medical treatment and self-care, excellent emotional support and coping skills, feeling that there is purpose for their life, and having a positive outlook.

Let's take a closer look at these four aspects of your health and where you invest your energy.

Physical: When most people think of health, they think of physical health first. Healthy nutrition and an active lifestyle are part of physical health—but there is much more. For optimal

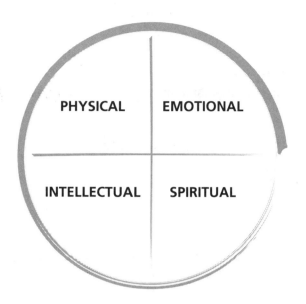

physical health, your primary needs for shelter, safety, and security must be met. Physical health is also related to the environment where you live and meeting your biologic needs such as sleep and rest. Physical health is important because it gives you the vitality to do what you need and want to do.

Emotional: This area of health includes the ability to accurately identify and cope with your feelings. Optimal emotional health does not mean being perfectly happy but rather, embracing the full spectrum of emotions for the depth and richness they bring to your life. An important part of emotional wellness is having satisfying relationships with others, healthy personal boundaries, and well-developed, self-nurturing skills.

Intellectual: Your intellectual side examines situations logically and values learning. For optimal intellectual health, challenge, growth, creativity, stimulation, and a sense of accomplishment are all important. From a practical standpoint, your thoughts have a powerful impact on your overall health.

Spiritual: Spirituality is a sense of connection and purpose. For some this may include religion but it is really much more than that. It is knowing that who you are is not defined by your possessions, your accomplishments, or even your contributions, but that you are worthy of love just as you are. It is the awareness that there is something greater than yourself and that there is a purpose for your life.

Remember Angie and Tom in Chapter 1? Tom shared his thoughts on what makes him feel healthy.

I know that what I eat affects my physical health but I can't imagine letting it rule my life. It's just food. What really makes me feel great is doing the things I love. I love spending time with Angie—laughing about our culinary disasters or sharing the challenges of our day. I love climbing to the top of a mountain and looking out as far as the eye can see. In those moments I experience both a sense of awe and an incredible sense of peace. To me, that is optimal health.

Where Does Your Energy Go In an Over Eating Cycle?

The Over Eating Cycle can lead to unnecessary weight gain, decreased pleasure in eating, decreased metabolism, and physical and emotional discomfort. When you eat primarily in response to triggers other than hunger, or if food is one of your major sources of pleasure or comfort, it may be difficult to build optimal health. Importantly, experiencing a void or unresolved turmoil in one or more of these other areas of your life may also make it more difficult to reach or maintain a healthier weight.

Physical: When hunger doesn't initiate your desire to eat, your body probably doesn't need the fuel so it will save the extra as fat. When you eat for reasons other than hunger, you are more likely to choose fun foods and comfort foods and less likely to choose foods with optimal nutrient content. Furthermore, when you are not eating to satisfy your physical need for food, you are more likely to overeat. In addition, if you lead a sedentary lifestyle, you may have less energy and your physical health will be less than optimal.

Emotional: Food and eating are sometimes used as a substitute for healthy coping skills and communication. For example, many people eat to literally stuff their anger. If anger is not expressed in a healthy manner, it can become destructive to the individual and their relationships. Or, if you eat half of a package of chocolate chip cookies because you are lonely, you will still be lonely when you are finished eating—but you will be stuffed too. To make matters worse, you may feel bad about yourself when you eat this way, and this can trigger more emotional eating. Another very important reality is that food can give only temporary relief from stress and difficult emotions. When emotions are not addressed in a healthy manner, they will continue to feed into unhealthy coping mechanisms—so the Over Eating Cycle continues.

Intellectual: People with weight issues may come to believe that their overeating is illogical and therefore, out of control. They generally know that they shouldn't eat so much but may instead find themselves thinking about food much of the time.

Spiritual: The spiritual part of you strives to find inner peace, unity, and a greater purpose for living. Overeating does not usually lead to inner peace or harmony, and may distract some people from fulfilling their higher purpose.

Think about Alicia and Paul from Chapter 1. They were trapped in an Over Eating Cycle but realized that it was not bringing them optimal health. Here's what Alicia said:

> *I was worried about how my weight was starting to affect my health. I was tired most of the time and I usually didn't have enough energy to exercise. But I also see that my intellectual energy was tied up in thinking about food so much. I was either wanting to eat or thinking bad things about myself for eating. And now I know that when I ate because of stress or other feelings, I really wasn't meeting my emotional needs either. This endless cycle was zapping me of the energy I needed to live the life I deserve.*

Where Does Your Energy Go In a Restrictive Eating Cycle?

Diets and other restrictive means of losing weight often don't address your whole self either. You have essential emotional, intellectual, and spiritual facets of your life that are all interconnected to your relationship with food. Any diet or weight loss program that doesn't address these other important parts of you (or worse yet, attempts to sever those connections) will ultimately fail, simply because human beings are multidimensional creatures.

Think about your past attempts at weight loss. What went wrong? Did you feel like you were struggling to overcome your urges to eat? If a diet worked temporarily, but failed to provide lasting results, what got in the way? Besides disrupting your body's physical balance, did your diet seem to clash with other important aspects of your life? You may have never considered this before, but is it possible that dieting ignored your need to balance the physical, emotional, intellectual, and spiritual aspects of your being? Let's explore this idea a little further.

Physical: Most diets focus on your physical being through diet and exercise but deal with the rest by simply saying, "It has to be a lifestyle change" (which usually translates to "You'll be on this diet for the rest of your life!") Sometimes the rules aren't even particularly healthy because they limit important nutrients. Ironically, chronic under-eating can have a detrimental affect on your metabolism and your energy level.

Emotional: Many people have strong emotional connections to food. Restaurants, holidays, and vacations are full of tempting "bad" foods that you aren't supposed to eat so you have to make a choice—the diet or the fun. While dieting, you may have felt sad or even angry that you weren't allowed to eat the foods you enjoyed. Sharing meals and food with other people becomes more difficult so you may start to dread those gatherings because they conflict with the rules of your diet. When your family, friends, and co-workers don't have to follow the same rules, you may feel awkward, angry, or left out so you may reach a point when trying to lose weight doesn't seem worth it. Most importantly, since many of your urges to eat may have been triggered by your emotions, you probably recognized that these urges didn't go away simply by imposing a strict set of rules.

Intellectual: A narrow, dogmatic diet is counterintuitive to your sensible, grounded nature. After all, attempting to lose weight by doing something that you know you cannot continue doing for the rest of your life just doesn't make sense. Your intellectual nature seeks personal and professional growth but over-analyzing and worrying about every eating decision limits your productivity and efficiency. Furthermore, restrictive diets may rob you of the energy needed to maintain concentration, endurance, and stamina.

Spiritual: Dieting requires a tremendous amount of energy and often leads to inner turmoil, guilt, and a sense of disconnection from the way things were intended to be. What could feel less natural and further from spirituality than eating in a manner that leaves you feeling weak, depressed, and even angry?

Trying to ignore these other aspects of living while dieting may have caused you to feel out of balance or out of sync with your own life. Karen from Chapter 1 who was caught in a Restrictive Eating Cycle felt this way:

> *I thought I was just trying to be healthy and look better. Now I am not so sure that what I was putting myself through was healthy at all. Most of my energy went toward trying to reach an arbitrary weight and hating my body. It didn't dawn on me that I would never find happiness by reaching a certain dress size—and that my life was passing me by while I tried.*

Invest Your Energy to Build Your Optimal Health

Where is your energy going? Where would you like it to go? As you thought about the four components of optimal health, perhaps you recognized that there are areas worthy of your attention and energy. Here are a number of ideas for each area; choose just a few to start with.

Physical Health Strategies

- Focus on improving your health rather than on losing weight.

- Make small changes rather than trying to overhaul your entire life. Work through *Am I Hungry?* one section at a time.

- Be careful not to turn *Am I Hungry?* into a diet by trying to follow it perfectly or feeling guilty when you don't (no one does—and it is not necessary in order to be healthy.)

- Get a personal physician and have regular check-ups. Take care of your health needs and don't ignore new or unusual symptoms.

- Eat fresh, healthful, and interesting foods.

- Engage in enjoyable physical activities regularly.

- Limit your screen time. Instead of spending passive hours in front of the television or computer, do something active that will restore your energy.

- Get plenty of rest and adequate sleep so you will feel clear and refreshed.

- Give and receive physical affection.

- Treat yourself to a massage, manicure, pedicure, or facial. Take a hot bath or long shower to relax and unwind.

- Clear the physical clutter around you.

- Create a pleasant personal space for yourself. Include comfortable pillows, photographs, candles, music, or whatever makes you feel happy and calm.

- Plant a garden and grow fresh vegetables, herbs, or flowers.

- Spend time in nature walking, hiking, camping, or just sitting.

Emotional Health Strategies

- Spend quality time with your family and friends having fun and sharing.
- Build intimacy and emotional connections with your partner.
- Make new friends or renew old friendships.
- Volunteer and give back to your community by helping others.
- Set appropriate boundaries in your relationships. Letting other people know how far into your emotional space they can go creates healthier relationships.
- Assert yourself to let others know how you feel, what you think, and what you need. Accept that beyond this, you cannot control what other people feel, think, or do.
- Manage stress effectively. It is not possible or even desirable to eliminate stress but it is possible to learn to release and cope with stress.
- Practice forgiveness. Harboring anger and hurt is harmful and can eat up precious emotional energy.
- Be vulnerable. Let people who you trust see your imperfections and fears. This can deepen intimacy and free you from the need to be perfect.
- Seek counseling or therapy if needed for emotional support and to build coping skills.

Intellectual Health Strategies

- Examine your values and priorities, then set your short- and long-term goals.
- Recognize that your thoughts lead to your feelings that then lead to your actions. Challenge yourself to think positively and powerfully.
- Learn something new—a skill, trade, hobby, language, or anything you find interesting.

- Read frequently. Experience new genres outside of your usual preferences (for example, if you usually read romance novels, try mysteries or classic literature).
- Visit museums or other novel places.
- Do brain teasers and play challenging games—by yourself and with others.
- Be creative, especially if you do not ordinarily have an opportunity to express yourself creatively. Experiment with art, music, crafts, and hobbies.
- Take classes online or at your local community center or college.
- Expand or deepen your knowledge in your area of interest.
- Become an expert on something. Learn everything you can about an area then share that knowledge with others by writing, speaking, or teaching.
- Participate in stimulating discussion groups.
- Explore new occupational and career opportunities.
- Travel or even explore areas close to home.

Spiritual Health Strategies

- Practice mindfulness. Be fully present in whatever you are doing—eating, talking, working, or playing—to experience full pleasure, satisfaction, and meaning.
- Renew and restore yourself through prayer and meditation.
- Schedule time for your inner work. Know yourself, your values, your dreams, and your purpose.
- Define your guiding principles so you will have a clear path to follow.
- Reclaim your joy! Experiencing joy is possible even as you face challenges.
- Look for the good in others; it is there somewhere waiting to be discovered.

- Write in a personal journal to explore your deepest thoughts and feelings.
- Visit your place of worship (or find one).
- Read a Bible or other meaningful, inspirational works.
- Have an attitude of gratitude. Being thankful for even the smallest of things will remind you of all that you have.
- Practice kindness without any expectation of anything in return.
- Remember that you already have everything you need to live an abundant life.

These ideas will help you start thinking about where you can invest your energy. It worked for Alicia:

Alicia beamed as she told us, "Up until now, I was eating constantly, never stopping long enough to become hungry. Last night I found myself staring into the refrigerator looking for something to fill me up. I remembered what you said, so I asked myself, 'Am I hungry?' I had to admit that I wasn't, so I knew there must be something besides food that I needed. Suddenly, I thought of my oil paints that hadn't been touched for months. I threw on an old shirt, turned on some loud music, and painted for three hours straight! The thought of food didn't cross my mind again the whole evening. I didn't need to eat; I needed to create! And for the first time in a long time, I truly felt full."

Decide *where* you will invest your energy—physically, emotionally, intellectually, and spiritually—in order to build optimal health. It will help you free yourself from your Over Eating and Restrictive Eating Cycles because food will serve its true function—to fuel your full and satisfying life.

Fitness: Your Personalized Exercise Prescription

People often secretly wish for a miracle to end their struggles with their weight, but so far, none exists. However, if you could bottle exercise, you would have the closest thing there is to a wonder drug in weight management. Since you can't get it in a pill, you'll have to put in a little more time and effort, but look at its numerous benefits:

Brand Name: Exercise

Generic Names (Numerous effective generics available): aerobics, basketball, bike riding, body sculpting, dancing, hiking, housework, playing with children, racquetball, rowing, stretching, swimming, tennis, walking, walking the dog, weight lifting, working out, yard work, yoga, and others.

Indications: Shown to be very effective for weight management and relief of fatigue, stress, low self-esteem, insomnia, boredom, and symptoms of depression and anxiety. May prevent, improve, or delay the onset of the following conditions: overweight/obesity, diabetes, high blood pressure, high cholesterol, heart disease, some types of cancer, some forms of arthritis, fibromyalgia, premenstrual syndrome, constipation, addictions, and many other health problems.

Benefits: Increased energy and productivity, increased metabolism, weight loss, improved sense of well-being and appearance, better sleep patterns, improved appetite regulation, lower blood sugar, lower heart rate and blood pressure, higher HDL (good) cholesterol, improved blood sugar control, and reduced risk of cancer.

Side Effects: Patients report feeling stronger, healthier, and more youthful.

Precautions: You should consult with your physician first, especially if you have any chronic medical conditions or unexplained symptoms. If you develop unexpected shortness of breath, chest, jaw, neck, or arm pain or pressure, rapid or irregular heart rate, lightheadedness, pain, or any other unexplained symptoms, stop and seek immediate medical advice and attention.

Dosage: Start with small dosages taken most days of the week and increase gradually as tolerance develops. Dosage may be adjusted if necessary to accommodate other responsibilities. However, due to the many beneficial effects, consistent usage is very important. Choose among the numerous generic brands available and alternate brands as needed to improve overall level of fitness, maintain interest, and assure compliance.

WARNING: Likely to become habit-forming when used regularly!

With regular physical activity you feel less stressed, have more stamina, and manage your weight more easily. Look for opportunities to be more active in your daily activities and include cardiorespiratory, flexibility, and strength training exercise for all around fitness.

Take charge of your fitness program by recognizing that it takes time to establish new healthier habits. Keep it challenging and fun to keep yourself motivated to stay on track with your healthier lifestyle. Most importantly, personalize your fitness program so that it suits your lifestyle and preferences. By creating a plan you love, you will enjoy the many benefits of exercise forever.

Nutrition: Nourish Yourself

Asking the question "Am I hungry?" gives you insight into *why* you want to eat. When you are using your Hunger and Fullness cues and other Decision Points effectively, they guide you in making decisions about *when* and *how much* to eat. Your knowledge about nutrition essentials and your awareness of your personal preferences guide your choices about what to eat.

We have found that the most effective way to make permanent healthy lifestyle changes is to learn to eat according to your body's signals *and* eat as healthfully as possible without feeling deprived. This balance can be achieved when you regularly consider reliable nutrition information in making your food choices, while still having the freedom to eat any type of food without judging yourself or feeling guilty.

Choosing food in this manner will meet your natural need for nutrition *and* enjoyment. Let's take a closer look at these two goals.

Meeting Your Need for Nutrition

Here are some strategies for applying what you have learned to create a healthy lifestyle.

Remember that food fuels your body. The real purpose of eating is to provide your body with the energy and nutrients it needs to function at its best. Since your body is the finest, most complex machine ever built, it performs best and lasts longest with top-of-the-line fuel.

Take charge of your eating decisions. When it comes to eating for health, being in charge means taking personal responsibility for your food choices. This does not contradict the all-foods-fit principle. Being in charge means combining your knowledge of nutrition with your personal lifestyle and preferences to develop a system that works best for you and your overall health.

So how do you implement this in your daily life? Paul explains how he did it:

> *It was great knowing that I would never have to diet again. But that didn't mean I wasn't interested in eating more healthfully. When I learned more about carbohydrates, I wondered if I was meeting the daily recommendation for fiber. I wrote down everything I ate and was surprised that I was getting only about 10 grams of fiber a day—not even close to the recommended 25 to 30 grams a day. My "healthy" low-fat puffed rice cereal had less than one gram of fiber per serving! So the next time we went shopping, I looked for higher-fiber cereal and bought whole-wheat pasta, wild rice, and whole-grain bread. I was*

already eating a lot of vegetables but I switched to eating fruit instead of drinking juice. Within a month, I had gradually increased my fiber intake by almost 20 grams without adding any more food—in fact, I felt more full with less food. The other bonus was—and don't laugh—I noticed that my bowel movements were more regular. I just feel better eating this way.

As you make similar assessments and changes, you will reap many benefits from eating for optimal health. Food can be used to your advantage.

Eat for overall health, not just for weight management. It is important to understand that these are not the same thing. In fact, as long as you eat fewer calories than your body burns, you will lose weight no matter which foods you choose. However, your physical health and vitality would suffer if you chose to eat only potato chips and candy bars—or for that matter, just lettuce and apples.

Eating like that would violate the principles of balance, variety, and moderation. More importantly, it is unlikely that your body's innate wisdom would tell you to eat that way for any prolonged period of time.

Make the healthiest choices you can without feeling deprived. At home and work, you will want to keep plenty of delicious healthy choices on hand to choose from when you get hungry. It is also very helpful to learn to prepare healthy foods in interesting, delicious ways and learn to prepare your favorites in healthier ways whenever possible. While eating out, this may mean choosing a great salad over a burger or asking to substitute a healthier choice for a less-healthy side dish with your favorite meal. Or, you may decide to skip the fried appetizers and just enjoy the main course. There are many options for delicious healthy foods if you are determined to make the best possible choices you can without feeling deprived.

Notice what happens when you eat. Check in with how you feel after you eat. Notice how long certain foods stay with you, whether you feel sluggish or more energetic after eating certain foods, and whether any foods cause uncomfortable symptoms. To put this into practical terms, here is what Beverly noticed:

> *I woke up late on Monday. I grabbed a cup of coffee with cream and sugar and headed out the door. On my way to work I noticed I was hungry but I realized that I had been in such a hurry that I had left my breakfast on the counter at home. I ate a glazed doughnut when I got to work. An hour later my hunger pangs came back so I had a glass of orange juice. It seemed like I was hungry all morning. I had trouble concentrating and I felt irritable.*

What was going on? That morning Beverly had consumed low-fiber carbohydrates, some fat, and an insignificant amount of protein. As a result, her blood sugars were intermittently rising rapidly, causing a quick and forceful insulin response to bring her blood sugar levels back to normal. If Beverly was to continue this pattern of eating, this spike and drop of her blood sugars could go on all day.

> *On Tuesday, I woke up in time to have a cup of coffee and a small whole-wheat bagel with peanut butter. I didn't get hungry again for over three hours. I ate a turkey sandwich and a cup of vegetable soup for lunch, and almonds and grapes in the middle of the afternoon. I felt great all day.*

What could have been responsible for the difference? The bagel, containing more starch and fiber than the simple carbohydrates in the doughnuts, along with the fat and protein from the peanut butter helped slow down the rise in her blood sugar and her subsequent insulin response. This resulted in a more stable blood sugar, which contributed to her improved mood, attention, performance, and less hunger.

This is just one example of how paying attention to the way your body responds to certain types and amounts of food will help you feel your best and meet your nutritional needs. It is important to explore your own eating habits to learn how to feed your body in a way that results in optimal health.

Resist restrictive diets. Without a doubt, you will continue to hear about many diets that promise amazing results. You may even be tempted to try one. Before you do, carefully examine the premise and science behind it. A good rule of thumb is, if it sounds too good to be true, it is! Linda learned this lesson and shared it with the group:

> *I loved being in charge of my eating and I was seeing steady progress in the way I looked and felt. However, when my daughter announced that she was getting married in two months, I decided I needed to do something more drastic to lose weight for the wedding. Someone at work was selling diet shakes and supplements so I spent about $80 on a two-week supply. I lost 4 pounds in 10 days—but I gained back 5 before the wedding! It took me a couple of months to get back on track again. I decided that next time I want to speed up my weight loss, I will bump up my exercise and work a little harder on eating fewer sweets and more vegetables.*

Be open to dietary guidance if needed. There is nothing wrong with making a decision to follow a specific dietary plan—after all, you are in charge. It is sensible to explore new ways of eating that are sound and make sense. You may have a medical reason for following a specific dietary plan or find that you need more structure and predetermined limits in order to lose weight. Just be sure to let hunger, satisfaction, and common sense guide you. A good rule of thumb here is, if you can't imagine eating a certain way for the rest of your life, then don't bother doing it for even a day. Robert used the structure of a diet plan to help him.

> *I understood the instinctive eating process but I was still having difficulty staying on track so I wasn't losing weight. Although I could never stick with a diet for long before, I decided to try one again, this time using my hunger signals to guide me. What a difference! I used the diet to help me choose what foods to eat but I didn't starve or deprive myself. I really feel that I am learning what it takes to manage my weight for life.*

Continue to educate yourself about nutrition. Without a doubt, science will continue to discover new important information about nutrition and health. In fact, things are changing so rapidly in this field that even credible information from reliable sources may evolve and change over time.

It is important that you find accurate and authoritative sources of nutrition information and keep yourself up to date. As an example, if your sister discovered that she has breast cancer and you decided to so some research, you would learn about scientific studies that show a link between high fat intake and breast cancer. You might then decide that it would be worthwhile to lower your own fat intake. By taking charge of your eating decisions and staying informed, you will have the flexibility and information you need to modify your eating habits to be the most beneficial for you.

Further, be sure to examine how the information you learn applies to your life. Just because you hear or read something, doesn't automatically mean you need to make a change in the way you eat if you are doing well. Your family doctor or a registered dietitian can help guide you through the maze of information that is available these days.

Meeting Your Need for Enjoyment

Let's face it. Food is wonderful. It is truly one of life's many pleasures. Realize that enjoying food is only a problem if it is your main source of pleasure. Let go of the guilt and make eating for enjoyment an intentional decision.

You may doubt that you can learn to freely choose to eat what you want without losing control if in the past you have vacillated between overeating and restrictive eating. But remember as you learn to eat instinctively again, you no longer have to be in control—just in charge.

The purpose of letting go of restrictive eating is to remove the false sense of value you place on certain foods. In essence, by letting go of the guilt, you eliminate the power that certain foods have over you so your desire to overeat them will diminish.

The key to eliminating guilt is to give yourself unconditional permission to eat any foods. This means that you place all foods on an even playing field where the choice to eat cake evokes no more guilt than the choice to eat an apple. In order to eat without guilt, strive to:

- Eliminate all judgments that certain foods are "good" while others are "bad."

- Eat what you really *want*, honoring your body's natural signals.

- Eat without having to pay penance (as in, "I'll eat this today, but I'll diet the rest of the week," or "I'll eat this now but I'll have to spend more time exercising tonight.").

Letting Go of Restrictive Eating

Despite the knowledge that deprivation leads to overeating, many people are still afraid to free themselves from dieting. Following are some of the common reasons people are reluctant to begin the process of taking charge of their eating:

"I won't make healthy choices." Fortunately this is not usually the case. When people are given free choice and access to a variety of foods, they tend to balance their intake to include mostly nutritious foods with smaller amounts of fun foods. That is because once you stop labeling foods as "good" or "bad," you will probably develop a greater appreciation for the taste of fresh healthful foods and not label them as diet foods. In addition, you will notice that you feel better physically and emotionally with a balance of nutritious foods, and your body will actually begin to crave them.

"I am *supposed* to feel guilty if I eat for enjoyment." Many popular food and diet ads feed into the erroneous concept that eating for pleasure is sinful and that you should strive to eat foods that are guilt-free. Choose food that will truly satisfy you—then allow yourself to fully enjoy your choice guilt-free.

"**I really shouldn't be eating this.**" Sometimes dieters only give themselves pseudo-permission to eat a particular food. They just temporarily allow themselves to eat a "bad" food, while in the back of their mind is the message, "I really shouldn't be eating this." Thus, instead of fully enjoying the food, they are already planning to pay penance for eating it by exercising, skipping a snack or a meal, or eating "light" to make up for it. Since they had never really given themselves permission to eat whatever they wanted in the first place, they continue to overeat, feel out of control, and punish themselves for it.

"**I'm afraid I'll never stop eating.**" At first you may experience an overwhelming fear that you won't be able to stop eating a particular food. Keep in mind that when you know that previously forbidden foods will always be allowed, the urgency to eat them in large quantities will eventually dissipate. Research has shown that people tire of eating the same kind of food over time, even foods they love. Some people find it helpful to go through food phases, where they try out one previously forbidden food at a time and eat it regularly until it loses its magic.

"**I know what will happen.**" Some people believe that they are addicted to certain foods and that eating even one bite of a certain food will trigger them to overeat. This becomes a self-fulfilling prophecy. They don't realize that depriving themselves of those foods caused the strong cravings and feeling of powerlessness around that food. Once they begin to eat one of these foods, their mind automatically prepares for a binge. Instead, follow the steps for eating without guilt and experiment with how your body responds to different foods and decide what foods you will choose to eat.

"**I am using the Hunger and Fullness Scale to control my eating.**" Feeling guilty when you eat if you are not hungry, or judging yourself for eating past a 5 or a 6 is no different from dieting. This form of restrictive eating will lead to the same deprivation-craving-overeating-guilt cycle. Instead, remember that you are in charge of your eating decisions. When you want to eat, ask yourself "Am I hungry?"—but you may choose to eat whether you are hungry or not. Since being in charge means taking responsibility, you are free to choose to eat or overeat if you want, as long as you acknowledge that there are consequences and you decide that for this situation, the consequences are worth it.

"I don't trust myself." A major obstacle to letting go of guilt is a lack of self trust. A history of cycling between overeating and restrictive eating can erode your trust in your ability to listen to your body's signals. The process of letting go of guilt is an important way to rebuild trust in your ability to be in charge of your decisions. Move through the strategies for eating without guilt at a pace that is comfortable for you.

Strategies For Eating Without Guilt

- Make a list of the foods that you enjoy, but that you generally restrict yourself from eating.

- Choose one of the "forbidden foods" from your list and give yourself permission to eat that food when you are hungry.

- When you are hungry and decide you want the food that you have chosen, purchase or prepare the amount you think you will need, or order one serving at a restaurant.

- Eat the food mindfully, without distractions, and focus on the aroma, appearance, flavor, and texture as you eat.

- Does the food taste as good as you imagined it would? Sometimes you will discover that the food is not as good as you thought it would be so you may decide not to finish it or decide that you won't bother with it in the future. If you do enjoy it, continue to give yourself permission to buy or order it whenever you want.

- You may decide to keep enough of the food in your house so that you know it will be there if you want it. However, for some people, keeping certain foods in the house can feel too scary. In that case, promise yourself that you will purchase and prepare only as much as you'll need for one sitting or that you will go to a restaurant and order that particular food when you want it.

- Don't be surprised if you want that food frequently at first. However, you will see that the cravings diminish when you realize that the food is no longer forbidden.

- Be aware of subtle messages that you may be giving yourself about eating these foods. Catch yourself when you begin thinking, "I shouldn't eat this," or "I'm going to eat it all in case I don't get another chance." Remember, all foods fit so you don't have to eat it all now.

- When you are ready, choose another food from your list and practice the process again.

- If you find yourself repeatedly overeating certain foods, review some of the earlier chapters for possible causes and solutions. By recognizing what is driving your overeating, you can take steps to address the issues.

- Repeat the process regularly to release yourself from the fear that you are not in charge of your eating. This process is also helpful if you find yourself obsessing about a particular food.

When you begin to give yourself unconditional permission to eat any foods, you will notice that food quickly loses the power and attraction it once held for you. You will begin to feel secure in the knowledge that you may choose among all of the wonderful food choices available when you are hungry, and that you don't have to stock up before you embark on your next round of self denial. Amazingly, you will also find yourself feeling more satisfied eating less food.

Nourishing Yourself

Striking the optimal balance between eating for nutrition and eating for enjoyment requires you to take charge of your eating decisions. Recall the tools you learned in earlier chapters for choosing what you will eat: when you are hungry, ask yourself, "What do I want? What do I need? What do I have?"

Then, use the principles of balance, variety, and moderation to look at the big picture.

Mitzi and Brad are well on their way to consistently meeting their needs:

> *We both love food and always thought that was what was keeping us from getting to a healthier weight. But now we are healthier and enjoying food even more. Mitzi took a Chinese cooking class at the community college and makes this amazing stir-fry with these unusual vegetables. Not to be outdone, I built a barbecue and Mitzi loves my grilled salmon with papaya salsa. I'm not saying that we don't still love chocolate cake. But now when we go out to dinner we share an entrée and one piece of cake between the two of us and that is plenty. I think the biggest difference is in our awareness of how the food we choose affects not only our weight, but how we feel—not to mention how healthy we are!*

Awareness is the most important tool for staying in charge. Whenever you recognize that you have gotten off track, notice which Decision Point you are at in the Eating Cycle. For example, you may have started eating because you were hungry and selected tasty, healthy food. However, if you became distracted and began to overeat, you could redirect yourself as soon as you noticed what you were doing. When you are aware of your thoughts, feelings, and actions, you can choose to return to Instinctive Eating at any point along the cycle.

Unlike dieting which may become more difficult over time, learning to eat instinctively again is a process that becomes easier with practice. Do not expect yourself to be perfect. It is not possible—and it is not necessary. Simply choose to use every opportunity to learn more about yourself and why, when, what, how, and how much you eat—and where you invest your energy.

Listening to your hunger cues, building a strong foundation of nutrition information, and choosing among all foods freely to meet your needs allows you to eat in a manner that nourishes your body, mind, and soul.

References

Albert, C. M., Hennekens, C. H., O'Donnell, C. J., Ajani, U. A., Carey, V. J., Willett, W.C., et al. (1998). Fish consumption and risk of sudden cardiac death. *Journal of the American Medical Association,* 279, 23-28.

American College of Sports Medicine. (2000). *ACSM's guidelines for exercise testing and prescription* (6th ed.). Baltimore: Lippincott Williams & Wilkins.

American College of Sports Medicine. (2001). *ACSM's resource manual for guidelines for exercise testing and prescription* (4th ed.). Baltimore: Lippincott Williams & Wilkins.

American Dietetic Association. (n.d.). *Food guide pyramid.* Retrieved October 27, 2003, from http://www.eatright.org/Public/NutritionInformation/92_fgp.cfm

American Heart Association. (n.d.). *Make healthy food choices.* Retrieved July 24, 2004, from http://www.americanheart.org/presenter.jhtml?identifier=537

American Heart Association. (n.d.). *Dietary guidelines.* Retrieved October 27, 2003, from http://www.americanheart.org/presenter.jhtml?identifier=1330

Anderson, J. W. (2003). Whole grains protect against atherosclerotic cardiovascular disease. *Proceedings of the Nutrition Society,* 62, 135-142.

Andlauer, W., Stehle, P., & Furst, P. (1998). Chemoprevention - A novel approach in dietetics. *Current Opinion in Clinical Nutrition and Metabolic Care,* 1, 539-547.

Barlow, C. E., Kohl, H. W., Gibbons, L. W., & Blair, S. N. (1995). Physical fitness, mortality, and obesity. *International Journal for Obesity Related Metabolic Disorders,* 19(4), S41-S44.

Barnes, P. M., & Schoenborn, C. A. (2003). *Physical activity among adults: United States, 2000: Advanced data from vital and health statistics.* Hyattsville, MD: National Center for Health Statistics.

Bazzano, L. A., He, J., Ogden, L. G., Loria, C. M., Vupputuri, S., Myers, L., et al. (2002). Fruit and vegetable intake and risk of cardiovascular disease in U.S. adults: The first National Health and Nutrition Examination Survey epidemiologic follow-up study. *American Journal of Clinical Nutrition,* 76, 93-99.

Bennett, W., & Gurin, J. (1982). *The dieter's dilemma: Eating less and weighing more.* New York: Basic Books, Inc.

Bilich, M. (2000). *Weight loss from the inside out: Help for the compulsive eater.* SelfHelpBooks.com.

Birch, L. L., & Fisher, J. O. (1996). The role of experience in the development of children's eating behavior. In E. Capaldi (Ed.), *Why we eat what we eat: The psychology of eating,* (pp. 133-137). Washington, DC: American Psychological Association.

Birch, L. L., Johnson, S. L., Andresen G., Peters, J. C., & Schulte, M. C. (1991). The variability of young children's energy intake. *New England Journal of Medicine,* 324, 232-235.

Blundell, J. E., & King, N. A. (1999). Physical activity and regulation of food intake: Current evidence. *Medicine and Science in Sports and Exercise,* 31(11), S573-S583.

Bowen, D. J., & Grunberg, N. H. (1990). Variations in food preference and consumption across the menstrual cycle. *Physiology & Behavior, 47*(2), 287-291.

Bray, G. A. (1969). Effect of caloric restriction on energy expenditure in obese patients. *Lancet,* 2, 397-398.

Bucher, H. C., Hengstler, P., Schindler, C., & Meier, G. (2002). N-3 polyunsaturated fatty acids in coronary heart disease: A meta-analysis of randomized controlled trials. *American Journal of Medicine,* 112, 298-304.

Canadian Society for Exercise Physiology. (2002). *Physical Activity Readiness Questionnaire: PAR-Q and You.* Retrieved August 13, 2004 from http://www.csep.ca/forms.asp

Carnethon, M. R., Gidding, S. S., Nehgme, R., Sidney, S., Jacobs, D. R., & Liu, K. (2003). Cardiorespiratory fitness in young adulthood and the development of cardiovascular disease risk factors. *Journal of the American Medical Association,* 290, 3092-3100.

Centers for Disease Control and Prevention. (2003, March 25). *Nutrition and physical activity: Recommendations.* Retrieved June 29, 2004, from http://www.cdc.gov/nccdphp/dnpa/physical/recommendations/index.htm

Centers for Disease Control and Prevention, National Center for Chronic Disease Prevention and Health Promotion. (1996). *Surgeon General's Report on Physical Activity and Health.* Atlanta, GA: CDC.

Center for Science in the Public Interest. (2003, January/February). Spin the bottle: How to pick a multivitamin [Electronic version]. *Nutrition Action Healthletter,* 30(1), 3-9. Retrieved July 24, 2004, from http://www.cspinet.org/nah/01_03/spin.pdf

Colditz, G. A. (1992). Economic costs of obesity. *American Journal of Clinical Nutrition,* 55, S503-S507.

Connolly, J., Romano, T., & Patruno, M. (1999). Selections from current literature: Effects of dieting and exercise on resting metabolic rate and implications for weight management. *Family Practice,* 16, 196-201.

Convertino, V. A., Armstrong, L. E., Coyle, E. G., Mack, G. W., Sawka, M. N., Senay, L. C., et al. (1996). American College of Sports Medicine position stand: Exercise and fluid replacement. *Medicine and Science in Sports and Exercise*, 28, i-vii.

Cotton, R. P. (1996). *Personal trainer manual: The resource for fitness professionals* (2nd ed.). San Diego: American Council on Exercise.

Coulston, A. M., & Peragallo-Dittko, V. (2004). Insulin resistance syndrome: A potent culprit in cardiovascular disease. *Journal of the American Dietetic Association*, 104, 176-179.

Craig, W., & Beck, L. (1999). Phytochemicals: Health protective effects. *Canadian Journal of Dietetic Practice and Research*, 60, 78-84.

Cummings, S., Parham, E. S., & Strain, G. W. (2002). Position of the American Dietetic Association: Weight management. *Journal of the American Dietetic Association*, 102, 1145-1155.

Dalton, S. (1997). *Overweight and weight management: The health professional's guide to understanding and practice*. Gaithersburg, MD: Aspen Publishers.

Davies, K. M., Heaney, R. P., Recker, R. R., Lampe, J. M., Barger-Lux, M. J., Rafferty, K., et al. (2000). Calcium intake and body weight. *Journal of Clinical Endocrinology & Metabolism*, 85(12), 4635-4638.

De Castro, J. M. (1988). Physiological, environmental, and subjective determinants of food intake in humans: a meal pattern analysis. *Physiology & Behavior*, 44, 651-659.

De Castro, J. M. (1990). Social facilitation of duration and size but not rate of the spontaneous meal intake of humans. *Physiology and Behavior*, 47, 1129-1135.

De Castro, J. M., & Brewer, E. M. (1991). The amount eaten in meals by humans is a power function of the number of people present. *Physiology and Behavior*, 51, 121-125.

Dischman, R. K., Washburn, R. A., & Heath, G. W. (2003). *Physical activity epidemiology*. Champaign, IL: Human Kinetics Publishers.

Dohm, F. A., Beattie, J. A., Aibel, C., & Striegel-Moore, R. H. (2001). Factors differing women and men who successfully maintain weight loss from women and men who do not. *Journal of Clinical Psychology*, 57(1), 105-117.

Donatelle, R., Snow, C., & Wilcox, A. (1999). *Wellness: Choices for health and fitness* (2nd ed.). Belmont, CA: Wadsworth Publishing Company.

Drewnowski, A. (1989). Sensory preferences for fat and sugar in adolescence and adult life. *Annals of the New York Academy of Sciences*, 561, 243-250.

Fernstrom, J. D., & Miller, G. D. (Eds.). (1994). *Appetite and body of weight regulation: Sugar, fat, and macronutrient substitutes*. Boca Raton, FL: CRC Press.

Field, A. E., Wing, R. R., Manson, J. E., Spiegelman, D. L. & Willett, W. C. (2001). Relationship of a large weight loss to long-term weight change among young and middle-aged U.S. women. *International Journal of Obesity*, 25, 1113-1121.

Fisher, J. O., & Birch, L.L. (2001). Early experiences with food and eating: Implications for the development of eating disorders. In J. K. Thompson & L. Smolak (Eds.), *Body image, eating disorders, and obesity in youth: Assessment, prevention, and treatment* (pp. 23-40). Washington, DC: American Psychological Association.

Fletcher, R. H., & Fairfield, K. M. (2002). Clinician's corner: Vitamins for chronic disease prevention in adults. *Journal of the American Medical Association*, 287, 3127-3129.

Folts, J. D. (2002). Potential health benefits from the flavonoids in grape products on vascular disease. *Advances in Experimental Medicine and Biology*, 505, 95-111.

Food and Nutrition Board. (1989). *Recommended Dietary Allowances* (10th ed., pp. 58-59). Washington: National Academy Press.

Ford, E. S., Mokdad, A. H., Giles, W. H., & Brown, D. W. (2003). The metabolic syndrome and antioxidant concentrations findings from the third National Health and Nutrition Examination Survey. *Diabetes*, 52, 2346-2352.

Freeland-Graves, J., & Nitzke, S. (2002). Position of the American Dietetic Association: Total diet approach to communicating food and nutrition. *Journal of the American Dietetic Association*, 102, 100-108.

Gaesser, G. (2002). *Big Fat Lies*. Carlsbad, CA: Gurze Books.

Gerstein, D. E., Woodward-Lopez, G., Evans, A. E., Klesey, K., & Drewnowski, A. (2004). Clarifying concepts about macronutrients' effects on satiation and satiety. *Journal of the American Dietetic Association*, 104, 1151-1153.

Goldfarb, A. H., & Jamurtas, A. Z. (1997). Beta-endorphin response to exercise: An update. *Sports Medicine*, 24(1), 8-16.

Goodpaster, B. H., He, J., Watkins, S., & Kelley, D. E. (2001). Skeletal muscle lipid content and insulin resistance: Evidence for a paradox in endurance-trained athletes. *Journal of Clinical Endocrinologic Metabolism*, 86, 5755-5761.

Grundy, S. M., Cleeman, J. I., Merz, C. N., Brewer, H. B., Jr., Clark, T., Hunninghake, D. B., et al. (2004). Implications of recent clinical trials for the National Cholesterol Education Program Adult Treatment Panel III guidelines. *Circulation*, 110, 227-239.

Gulati, M., Pandey, D. K., Arnsdorf, M.F., Lauderdale, D. S., Thisted, R. A., Wicklund, R. H., et al. (2003). Exercise capacity and the risk of death in women: The St. James Women Take Heart Project. *Circulation*, 108(13), 1554-1559.

Guyton, A. C., & Hall, J. E. (2000). *Textbook of medical physiology* (10th ed.). Philadelphia: W. B. Saunders Company.

Hansen, V., & Goodman, S. (1997). *The seven secrets of slim people.* Carlsbad, CA: Hay House Inc.

Hardman, A. E. (2001). Issues of fractionization of exercise (short vs. long bouts). *Medicine and Science in Sports and Exercise,* 33, S421-S427.

Hasler, C. M., Bloch, A. D., & Thomson, C. A. (2004). Position of the American Dietetic Association: Functional foods. *Journal of the American Dietetic Association,* 104, 814-826.

Heatherton, T. F., Herman, C. P., & Polivy, J. (1992). Effects of distress on eating: The importance of ego-involvement. *Journal of Personality and Social Psychology,* 62(5), 801-803.

Heber, D. (2004). Vegetables, fruits and phytoestrogens in the prevention of diseases. *Journal of Postgraduate Medicine,* 50, 145-149.

Herman, C. P., Polivy, J., Lank, C. N., & Heatherton, T. F. (1987). Anxiety, hunger, and eating behavior. *Journal of Abnormal Psychology,* 96(3), 264-269.

Hill, A. J., Weaver, C. F. L., & Blundell, J. E. (1991). Food craving, dietary restraint and mood. *Appetite,* 17, 187-197.

Hill, J., & Wing, R. (2003). *The National Weight Control Registry.* Retrieved September 27, 2003, from www.kaiserpermanente.org/medicine/permjournal/sum03/registry.html

Hirschmann, J., & Munter, C. (1988). *Overcoming overeating.* New York: Fawcette Columbine.

Hirschmann, J., & Zaphiropoulos, L. (1993). *Preventing childhood eating problems.* Carlsbad, CA: Gurze Books.

Hu, F. B. (2003). Plant-based foods and prevention of cardiovascular disease: An overview. *American Journal of Clinical Nutrition,* 78, 544S-551S.

Institute of Medicine. (2002). Dietary reference intakes for energy, carbohydrate, fiber, fat, fatty acids, cholesterol, protein, and amino acids. Retrieved July 24, 2004, from http://www.iom.edu/Object.File/Master/4/154/0.pdf

Jacqmain, M., Doucet, E., Després, J. P., Bouchard, C., & Tremblay, A. (2003). Calcium intake, body composition, and lipoprotein-lipid concentrations in adults. *American Journal of Clinical Nutrition,* 77, 1448-1452.

Jakicic, J. M., Marcus, B. H., Gallagher, K. I. (2003). Effect of exercise duration and intensity on weight loss in overweight, sedentary women: A randomized trial. *Journal of the American Medical Association,* 290, 1323-1330.

Johnston, L., Reynolds, H. R., Patz, M., Hunningshake, D. B., Schultz, K., & Westereng, B. (1998). Cholesterol-lowering benefits of a whole grain oat ready-to-eat cereal. *Nutrition in Clinical Care,* 1, 6-12.

Joshipura, K. J., Hu, F. B., Manson, J. E., Stampfer, M. J., Rimm, E. B., Speizer, F. E., et al. (2001). The effect of fruit and vegetable intake on risk for coronary heart disease. *Annals of Internal Medicine*, 134, 1106-1114.

Kano, S. (1989). *Making peace with food*. New York: Harper & Row.

Katherine, A. (1991). *Anatomy of a food addiction* (3rd ed.). Carlsbad, CA: Gurze Books.

Kesaniemi, Y. A., Danforth, E., Jensen, M. D., Kopelman, P. G., Lefebvre, P., & Reeder, B. A. (2001). Dose-response issues concerning physical activity and health: An evidence-based symposium. *Medicine and Science in Sports and Exercise*, 33, S351-S358.

Keys, A. (1950). *The biology of human starvation*. Minneapolis: University of Minnesota Press.

King, G. A., Herman, C. P., & Polivy, J. (1987). Food perception in dieters and non-dieters. *Appetite*, 8, 147-158.

Kleiner, S. M. (1999). Water: An essential but overlooked nutrient. *Journal of the American Dietetic Association*, 99, 200-206.

Kraemer, W. J., & Fleck, S. J. (1987). *Designing resistance training programs* (2nd ed.). Champaign, IL: Human Kinetics.

Krauss, R. M., Eckel, R. H., Howard, B., Appel, L. J., Daniels, S. R., Deckelbaum, R. J., et al. (2000). Revision 2000: A statement for healthcare professionals from the Nutrition Committee of the American Heart Association. *Journal of Nutrition*, 131(1), 132-146.

Kris-Etherton, P. M., Harris, W. S., & Appel, L. J. (2003). Fish consumption, fish oil, omega-3 fatty acids, and cardiovascular disease. *Circulation*, 106, 2747-2757.

Kuller, L. W. (1997). Dietary fat and chronic diseases: Epidemiologic overview. *Journal of the American Dietetic Association*, 97, S9-S15.

Laaksonen, D. E., Lakka, H-M., Salonen, J. T., Niskanen, L. K., Rauramaa, R., & Lakka, T. A. (2002). Low levels of leisure time physical activity and cardiorespiratory fitness predict development of the metabolic syndrome. *Diabetes Care*, 25, 1612-1618.

LaForge, R. (1995). Exercise-associated mood alterations: A review of interactive neurobiologic mechanisms. *Medicine, Exercise, Nutrition and Health*, 4(1), 17-32.

Lefevre, M., Kris-Etherton, P. M., Zhao, G., & Tracy, R. P. (2004). Dietary fatty acids, hemostasis, and cardiovascular disease risk. *Journal of the American Dietetic Association*, 104, 410-419.

Leinonen, K. S., Poutanen, K. S., & Mykkanen, H. M. (2000). Rye bread decrease serum total and LDL cholesterol in men with moderately elevated serum cholesterol. *The Journal of Nutrition*, 130, 164-171.

Lin, Y. C., Lyle, R. M., McCabe, L. D., McCabe, G. P., Weaver, C. M. & Teegarden, D. (2000). Dairy calcium is related to changes in body composition during a two-year exercise intervention in young women. *Journal of the American College of Nutrition*, 19(6), 754-760.

Liu, S., Manson, J. E., Lee, I., Cole, S. R., Hennekens, C. H., Willett, W. C., et al. (2000). Fruit and vegetable intake and risk of cardiovascular disease: The women's health study. *American Journal of Clinical Nutrition*, 72, 922-928.

Magnen, J. L. (1985). Hunger. Great Britain: Press Syndicate of the University of Cambridge.

Marlett, J. A., & Slavin, J. L. (1997). Position of the American Dietetic Association: Health implications of dietary fiber. *Journal of the American Dietetic Association*, 97, 1157-1159.

Maslow, A. H. (1954). *Motivation and personality*. New York: Harper

McInnis, K. J., Franklin, B. A., & Rippe, J. M. (2003). Counseling for physical activity in overweight and obese patients. *American Family Physician*, 67, 1249-1256.

Mela, D. J., & Rogers, P. J. (1998). Food, eating, and obesity: *The psychobiological basis of appetite and weight control*. London: Chapman & Hall.

Melanson, E. L., Sharp, T. A., Schneider, J., Donahoo, W. T., Grunwald, G. K., & Hill, J. O. (2003). Relation between calcium intake and fat oxidation in adult humans. *International Journal of Obesity*, 27, 196-203.

Mellin, L. (1997). *The solution*. New York: HarperCollins Publishers.

Mensink, R. P., Zock, P. L., Kester, A. D. M., Katan, M. B. (2003). Effects of dietary fatty acids and carbohydrates on the ratio of serum total to HDL cholesterol and on serum lipids and apolipoproteins: A meta-analysis of 60 controlled trials. *American Journal of Clinical Nutrition*, 77, 1146-1155.

Miller, G. D., Jarvis, J. K., & McBean, L. D. (2000). *Handbook of dairy foods and nutrition* (2nd ed.). Boca Raton, FL: CRC Press.

Miller, W. C., Koceja, D. M., & Hamilton, E. J. (1997). A meta-analysis of the past 25 years of weight loss research using diet, exercise or diet plus exercise intervention. *International Journal of Obesity*, 21, 941-947.

Mokdad, A. H., Serdula, M. K., Dietz, W. H., Bowman, B. A., Marks, J. S., & Koplan, J. P. (1999). The spread of the obesity epidemic in the United States, 1991-1998. *Journal of the American Medical Association*, 282, 1519-1522.

Morris, C. D., & Carson, S. (2003). Routine vitamin supplementation to prevent cardiovascular disease: A summary of the evidence for the U.S. Preventive Services Task Force. *Annals of Internal Medicine*, 139, 56-70.

Muller, H., Lindman, A. S., Brantsaeter, A. L., & Pedersen, J. I. (2003). The serum LDL/HDL cholesterol ratio is influenced more favorably by exchanging saturated with unsaturated fat than by reducing saturated fat in the diet of women. *Journal of Nutrition*, 133, 78-83.

National Alliance for Nutrition and Activity. (2002, June). From wallet to waistline: The hidden costs of super sizing. Retrieved July 26, 2004, from http://www.cspinet.org/new/pdf/final_price_study.pdf

National Heart, Lung, and Blood Institute. (2001). Expert panel on detection, evaluation, and treatment of high blood cholesterol in adults (Adult Treatment Panel III): Executive summary of the third report of the National Cholesterol Education Program (NCEP). *Journal of the American Medical Association*, 285, 2486-2497.

National Institutes of Health Technology Assessment Conference Panel. (1993). Methods for voluntary weight loss and control. *Annals for Internal Medicine*, 119, 764-770.

Nebeling, L., Rogers, C. J., Berrigan, D., Hursting, S., & Ballard-Barbash, R. (2004). Weight cycling and immunocompetence. *Journal of the American Dietetic Association*, 104(6), 892-894.

Newman, R. K., Newman, C. W., & Graham, H. (1989). The hypercholesterolemic function of barley beta-glucans. *Cereal Foods World*, 34, 883-886.

Orbach, S. (1978). *Fat is a feminist issue*. New York: Berkley Medallion Book.

Pate, R. R., Pratt, M., Blair, S. N., Haskell, W. L., Macera, C. A., Bouchard, C., et al. (1995). Physical activity and public health: A recommendation from the Centers for Disease Control and Prevention and the American College of Sports Medicine. *Journal of the American Medical Association*, 273(5), 402-407.

Pearson, L., & Pearson L. (1973). *The psychologist's eat anything diet*. New York: Peter H. 179 Publishers.

Pennington, J. A. T. (1998). *Bowes & Church's food values of portions commonly used* (17th ed.). Philadelphia: Lippincott.

Poehlman, E. T. (1989). A review: Exercise and its influence on resting energy metabolism in man. *Medicine and Science in Sports and Exercise*, 21(5), 515-525.

Polivy, J., & Herman, C. (1985). Dieting and binging: A causal analysis. *American Psychology*, 40(2), 193-201.

Pollock, M. L., Gaesser, G. A., Butcher, J. D., Despres, J., Dishman, R. K., Franklin, B. A., et al. (1998). American College of Sports Medicine position stand: Recommended quantity and quality of exercise for developing and maintaining cardiorespiratory and muscular fitness, and flexibility in healthy adults. *Medicine & Science in Sports & Exercise*, 30(6), 975-991.

Reddy, K. S., & Katan, M. B. (2004). Diet, nutrition and the prevention of hypertension and cardiovascular diseases. *Public Health Nutrition*, 7, 167-186.

Remington, D., Fisher, G., & Parent, E. (1983). *How to lower your fat thermostat.* Provo, UT: Vitality House International, Inc.

Richardson, D. P. (2003). Whole grain health claims in Europe. *Proceedings of the Nutrition Society,* 62, 161-169.

Ripsin, C. M., Keenan, J. M., Jacobs, D., Elmer, P. J., Welch, R. R., Van Horn, L., et al. (1992). Oat products and lipid lowering: A meta-analysis. *Journal of the American Medical Association,* 267, 3317-3325.

Rissanen, T. H., Voutilainen, S., Virtanen, J. K., Venho, B., Vanharanta, M., Mursu, M., et al. (2003). Low intake of fruits, berries and vegetables is associated with excess mortality in men: The Kuopio Ischaemic Heart Disease Risk Factor (KIHD) Study. *Journal of Nutrition,* 133(1), 199-204.

Robinson, B. E., Gjerdingen, D. K., & Houge, D. R. (1995). Obesity: A move from traditional to more patient-oriented management. *Journal of the American Board of Family Physicians,* 8, 99-108.

Rolls, B. J., & Rolls, E. T. (1982). *Thirst.* Great Britain: Press Syndicate of the University of Cambridge.

Roth, G. (1984). *Breaking free from compulsive eating.* New York: New American Library.

Roth, G. (1989). *Why weight? A guide to ending compulsive eating.* New York: New American Library.

Sallis, J. F. (1994, August). *Influences on physical activity of children, adolescents, and adults.* Retrieved July 24, 2004, from http://www.fitness.gov/influences.pdf

Satter, E. M. (1986). The feeding relationship. *Journal of the American Dietetic Association,* 86(3), 352-356.

Satter, E. M. (1987). *How to get your kid to eat ... but not too much.* Palo Alto, CA: Bull Publishing Company.

Satter, E. M. (1996). Internal regulation and the evolution of normal growth as the basis for prevention of obesity in children. *Journal of the American Dietetic Association,* 96(9), 860-864.

Schwartz, B. (1996). *Diets don't work.* Houston: Breakthru Publishing.

Scott, C. L. (2003). Diagnosis, prevention, and intervention for the metabolic syndrome. *American Journal of Cardiology,* 3, 35i-42i.

Shade, E. D., Ulrich, C. M., Wener, M. H., Wood, B., Yasui, Y., Lacroix, K., et al. (2004). Frequent intentional weight loss is associated with lower natural killer cell cytotoxicity in postmenopausal women: Possible long-term immune effects. *Journal of the American Dietetic Association,* 104(6), 903-912.

Shils, M. E., Olson, J. A., Shike, M. Lea, & Febiger. (1994). *Modern Nutrition in Health and Disease,* (8th ed.). Philadelphia: Publisher.

Skinner, J. D., Bounds, W., Carruth, B. R., & Ziegler, P. (2003). Longitudinal calcium intake is negatively related to children's body fat indexes. *Journal of the American Dietetic Association,* 103(12), 1626-1631.

Slavin, J. (2003). Why whole grains are protective: Biological mechanisms. *Proceedings of the Nutrition Society*, 62, 129-134.

Sothern, M. S., & Gordon, S. T. (2003). Prevention of obesity in young children: A critical challenge for medical professionals. *Clinical Pediatrics*, 42, 101-111.

Stagnitti, M. N. (2001) Statistical brief #34: The prevalence of obesity and other chronic health conditions among diabetic adults in the U.S. community population. Retrieved June 28, 2004, from http://www.meps.ahrq.gov/papers/st34/stat34.pdf

Stunkard, A. J., & Wadden, T.A. (1992). Psychological aspects of severe obesity. *American Journal of Clinical Nutrition*, 55, 524S-32S.

Tribole, E., & Resch, E. (1995). *Intuitive Eating*. New York: St. Martin's Press.

U.S. Department of Agriculture. (1996, October). *The food guide pyramid*. Retrieved July 19, 2004, from www.usda.gov/cnpp/pyrabklt.pdf

U.S. Department of Health and Human Services. (2004, March) *Effects of omega-3 fatty acids on cardiovascular disease: Summary*. Retrieved May 10, 2004, from http://www.ahrq.gov/clinic/epcsums/o3cardsum.pdf

U.S. Department of Health and Human Services. (2004, May 27). The Surgeon General's Call to Action to Prevent and Decrease Overweight and Obesity: *Overweight and obesity: At a glance*. Retrieved June, 29, 2004, from http://www.surgeongeneral.gov/topics/obesity/calltoaction/fact_glance.htm

U.S. Department of Health and Human Services and U.S. Department of Agriculture. (2000, May 30). *Nutrition and your health: Dietary guidelines for Americans* (5th ed.). Retrieved October 27, 2003, from http://health.gov/dietaryguidelines/dga2000/document/frontcover.htm

U.S. Food and Drug Administration. (1999, May 17). *The food label*. Retrieved July 25, 2004, from http://www.fda.gov/opacom/backgrounders/foodlabel/newlabel.html

U.S. National Library of Medicine and The National Institutes of Health. (2003, October 17). *Caffeine in the diet*. Retrieved July 24, 2004, from http://www.nlm.nih.gov/medlineplus/ency/article/002445.htm

Wadden, T. A., & Stunkard, A. J. (Eds.). (2002). *Handbook of obesity treatment*. New York: The Guilford Press.

Wardlaw, G. M. (1997). *Contemporary Nutrition* (3rd ed.). Dubuque, IA: Brown and Benchmark Publishers.

Wargovich, M. J. (1999). Nutrition and cancer: The herbal revolution. *Current Opinion in Clinical Nutrition and Metabolic Care*, 2, 421-424.

Waterhouse, D. (1996). *Outsmarting the female fat cell.* Portland, ME: Waterhouse Publications.

Weinberg, R. S., & Gould, D. (2003). *Foundations of sport and exercise psychology.* (3rd ed.). Champaign, IL: Human Kinetics Publishers.

Wheeler, M. L. (2003). Nutrient database for the 2003 exchange lists for meal planning. *Journal of the American Dietetic Association,* 103, 894-920.

White, S. (2002). Exercise can help insomniacs. *IDEA Personal Trainer,* 13(10), 10.

Whitney, E. N., & Rolfes, S. R. (2002). *Understanding Nutrition* (9th ed.). Belmont, CA: Wadsworth Group.

Wildman, R. E. C., & Medeiros, D. M. (2000). *Advanced human nutrition.* Boca Raton, FL: CRC Press.

Wing, R. R. (1999) Physical activity in the treatment of the adulthood overweight and obesity: Current evidence and research issues (Roundtable Consensus Statement). *Medicine and Science in Sport and Exercise,* 31, S547-S552.

Woods, S. C., Seeley, R. J., Porte, D. J., & Schwartz, M. W. (1998). Signals that regulate food intake and energy homeostasis. *Science,* 280, 1378-1383.

Zemel, M. B., Thompson, W., Milstead, A., Morris, K., & Campbell, P. (2004). Calcium and dairy acceleration of weight and fat loss during energy restriction in obese adults. *Obesity Research,* 12(4), 582-590.

About the Author and Collaborators

Michelle May, M.D.

Michelle May, M.D. is a board certified family physician and a recovered yoyo dieter. She developed the Am I Hungry? multidimensional, cognitive-behavioral weight management program in collaboration with Psychologist Lisa Galper, and a registered dietitian and an exercise physiologist. Dr. May has spoken widely on this innovative approach to weight management at hundreds of medical conferences, hospitals, corporate wellness programs, health clubs, spas, schools, and community organizations. Her follow-up book, *I'm Not Hungry; What Now?* will be published in 2005. She is also co-author of the children's book, *"H" is for Healthy – Weight Management For Kids.*

Dr. May earned her bachelor's degree in psychology from Arizona State University and her medical degree from the University of Arizona College of Medicine. She completed a three-year family practice residency at Good Samaritan Medical Center in Phoenix, Arizona and has been in private practice in a Phoenix suburb since 1991.

She has served as the chairperson for the Subcommittee on Women and in the Congress of Delegates of the 93,000-member American Academy of Family Physicians. She was elected president of the Arizona Academy of Family Physicians and actively participates in the Arizona Department of Health Services Obesity Prevention Program. She is a recognized leader in many other professional and community organizations.

Dr. May must practice what she preaches in order to balance her personal and professional life while maintaining her own optimal health. She cherishes her relationships with her two children, Tyler and Elyse, and regularly enjoys walking, hiking, and yoga. She and her husband, Owen, a chef, share a passion for gourmet and healthful cooking, wine tasting, and traveling.

Lisa Galper, Psy.D.

Lisa Galper, Psy.D. is a licensed clinical psychologist specializing in eating disorders, compulsive overeating, and weight management. For the past 15 years, she has devoted herself to teaching people how to step off the diet roller coaster and replace destructive eating patterns with truly effective tools for lifelong weight management. Dr. Galper has a strong commitment to challenging widespread cultural messages that perpetuate the myth that it is necessary to struggle against our own bodies in order to lose weight. Her passion for this work arose out of her own journey to victory over diet and weight obsession and compulsive overeating.

Dr. Galper has earned a reputation as one of the foremost experts in weight management in the Phoenix area. In addition to collaborating with Dr. Michelle May in the development of the Am I Hungry? program, she is currently the chief psychologist for the Balance program at Scottsdale Healthcare, and has worked with the Weight For Life program facilitating behavioral aftercare groups for bariatric surgery patients. In addition, she is the designer and instructor of the behavioral education classes at Scottsdale Bariatric Center. Dr. Galper maintains a private practice in Scottsdale, Arizona. In her free time she indulges her passion for travel, exploring other cultures, and spending time with her wonderful and supportive friends and family.

Janet K. Carr, M.S., R.D.

Janet Carr, M.S., R.D., is a registered dietitian specializing in weight management and eating disorders since 1998. Her intuitive understanding and passion for sharing a non-diet approach derives from her personal battle with eating and weight.

With an undergraduate degree in education from Bob Jones University and a master's degree in nutrition from the University of Alabama, Janet's training and experience provide the ideal combination for her frequent role as a nutrition therapist and educator. As a staff dietitian and former director of nutrition services at Remuda Ranch Programs for Anorexia and Bulimia, the largest inpatient facility for girls and women struggling with eating disorders, Janet worked closely with persons struggling with issues and behaviors surrounding food and weight.

When not working as an outpatient dietitian in the Blacksburg, Virginia area, Janet spends her leisure time in her herb garden, cooking, and playing with her young son, Hudson. She also enjoys hiking, kayaking, and camping with her husband, Doug.

Paul St. Onge, M.S.

With a Bachelor's degree in Psychology from LeMoyne College, and a Master's degree in Kinesiology from Arizona State University, Paul St. Onge, M.S. is pursuing his Doctorate in Biomechanics and Human Performance at Auburn University. Paul combines his knowledge of psychology and fitness to encourage others to achieve optimal health. He plans to teach and conduct scientific research on physical activity and health throughout the lifespan.

Loraine Parish, M.S.

Loraine Parish, M.S. is pursuing a Doctoral degree in Motor Development at Auburn University. While focusing her studies on physical activity and sport motivation, Loraine earned a Bachelor's degree in Exercise Science from Auburn University and a Master's degree in Sport Psychology from Arizona State University. Loraine embodies the benefits of increased health, fitness, and wellness. After completing her Doctorate, Loraine will continue to educate and motivate others in the prevention of obesity and chronic diseases through the adoption of healthier behaviors.

Please visit our website:
www.AmIHungry.com

- Register to receive a complimentary subscription to our *Am I Hungry?* E-newsletter
  - Motivational articles
  - Inspiring stories
  - Great resources
  - Delicious healthy recipes
  - Educational materials
  - Latest research
  - Links to useful websites
  - And much more!
- Participate in *Am I Hungry?* Workshops and Teleseminars
- Find more practical tools for coping with your eating triggers effectively in *I'm Not Hungry—What Now?*
- Register for *Am I Hungry?* programs and special events
- Arrange to have Michelle May, M.D. present at your conference or event
- Become a trained and licensed *Am I Hungry?* Facilitator
- View additional products, resources, articles, and website links
- Purchase this book at special quantity discounts for promotions, fund raising, or educational use